IRAQ:

People of Promise,
Land of Despair

IRAQ:
People of Promise, Land of Despair

Canon Andrew White

Sovereign World Limited

PO Box 777
Tonbridge
Kent, TN11 0ZS
United Kingdom

Unless otherwise indicated, all scripture quotations are from the New International Version, inclusive language version, copyright the International Bible Society 1999; published by Hodder and Stoughton.

ISBN: 1 85240 350 0

The publishers aim to produce books which will help to extend and build up the Kingdom of God. We do not necessarily agree with every view expressed by the author, or with every interpretation of Scripture expressed. We expect each reader to make his/her judgement in the light of their own understanding of God's Word and in an attitude of Christian love and fellowship.

Cover design by CCD, www.ccdgroup.co.uk
Typeset by CRB Associates, Reepham, Norfolk
Printed by Clays Ltd, St Ives plc

Dedication

*This book is dedicated to
the millions of suffering Iraqi children,
both living and departed;
especially Ahmed and Immanuel,*

*and to my sons
Josiah and Jacob*

*and also to my godchildren
Alexander Muir, Leilani Bliss Deon Locket-Haney,
Mark and Oliver Roberts, Sasha Watson, Alice Cross,
Hanna Rivka Thomas and Toby Ralph*

Acknowledgments

In any work which involves risk taking one always needs a team. I have been blessed with a most amazing group of people who have been prepared to stand besides me in the most difficult of circumstances. My family have always been prepared to share me with those in great need. Especially my wife Caroline and sons Josiah and Jacob who make great sacrifices for the sake of reconciliation. I remain eternally grateful to my spiritual mentor the late Lord Donald Coggan, former Archbishop of Canterbury who taught me to take risks and not care. Lord Carey of Clifton the former Archbishop of Canterbury has also been a tower of support and has shown great commitment to the search for a long-term peace in the Middle East.

Then there is Georges Hormis Sada, our brother in Baghdad, who loves his people and nation and has been prepared to take great risks for the sake of reconciliation. Brother Georges as he is known, is the President of the Evangelical Church in Iraq and the former Air vice Marshall. Without Georges there would be no story.

My Bishop Colin Bennetts has supported me and released me to do this work. He has travelled with me on that long and difficult road to Baghdad. I could not have continued this work without my dear friend and colleague Tom Kay-Shuttleworth who accompanied me on most of this difficult work. Then there were the many people back in Coventry providing the back up and support. Lynne and Karl Griffiths-Fulton, Muriel Stubbins, Yvette McDonald, Veronica Meredith, Richard Hathaway, Alexander Chance, Michelle Berry, Hannah King, Sue Bourne, Jens, Ewelina, Andrej, Nina, Don Lindon, David and Francis Hawkey, Pat Holmes, Joachim von Koielichen, Oliver Schugraff, Court Clarkson and Edith Adejobi. I am also grateful to all those who over the years have dared to travel with me, especially Lord Simon Reading one of the patrons of the International Centre for Reconciliation.

I would also like to thank the countless number of people who supported our work in Iraq and especially those who enabled the Bone Marrow Transplant programme to take place including, Sir Richard Branson, CAFOD, Medical Aid for Iraqi Children and Dr Tony Darbyshire at the Birmingham Children's Hospital. I do not forget those people who helped us in the very early days especially Stephen, Jose, Riad and Patrick. And then there is the former Provost of Coventry The Very Rev'd John Petty, who every day encouraged me to keep taking risks along with my predecessor Canon Paul Oestreicher. I continue to thank my clerical colleagues past and present at Coventry Cathedral, who not only have always encouraged me but have had to regularly pick up commitments that I left behind in Coventry: Canons Vivian Faull, Chris Burch, Stewart Beak, David Robinson, Justin Welby and our present Dean the Very Rev'd John Irvine.

I would also like to thank my Iraqi friends in England, Karen, Wafir and Sajad Al Ghabban, John Alpha and Dr Mudhafa Amin. Though away from there motherland they have not forgotten their people and have helped me to help those left behind in that great land of the Euphrates and Tigris. Ultimate thanks must go to the people of Iraq who have been prepared to share both the joy and great pain of their life with me.

Thanks must also go to David Chancellor who also travelled with me and took the photographs and Sue Cutter who has not just managed to organise my life but has also checked this script. Finally I thank the Master and Fellows of Clare College Cambridge for my appointment as Eric Lane Fellow, a position that gave me the opportunity to produce this little book in a very limited space of time.

About the author

Canon Andrew is the Director of the International Centre for Reconciliation (ICR) at Coventry Cathedral. He is responsible for the management of the Centre and its practical conflict resolution and prevention work in the Middle East. Much of his time is spent in some of the world's gravest areas of conflict, including Iraq, Israel and Palestine, and northern Nigeria.

As Director of the ICR, Canon Andrew is also responsible for the Community of the Cross of Nails. This is a world-wide network of almost 250 organisations in 60 different countries committed to reconciliation, which is co-ordinated from Coventry Cathedral.

Canon Andrew is one of world's leading experts on Middle Eastern affairs, with a particular insight into Jewish-Christian relations. In 2001, he was appointed by George Carey, Archbishop of Canterbury 1990 to 2002 as his Special Representative to the Middle East after his role in brokering the historic Alexandria Declaration, which was the first time that the leaders of the Christian, Jewish and Muslim faith communities in Israel/Palestine had ever signed an agreement to work together for peace in the Holy Land. Today, the so-called Alexandria Process – which uses religious leaders to augment the political peace process – is one of the only continuing and viable avenues through which senior Israeli and Palestinian religious and political leaders can continue to meet together.

Before ordination, Canon Andrew studied anaesthetics and surgery and worked as an Operating Department Practitioner at St Thomas' Hospital, London. His interest in Christian-Jewish matters began while he was a postgraduate student at Ridley Hall, Cambridge, where he became the founding President of the Cambridge University Jews and Christians society. Since that time, he has developed a specialised knowledge of the role of Israel in Christian theologies, and has written extensively on the subject.

Prior to his appointment to Coventry Cathedral – at that time he was the youngest Canon in the Church of England – Canon Andrew was a vicar in Clapham, London. He combined his parish duties with being a Councillor in the Borough of Wandsworth, and deputy chairman of Social Services.

Canon Andrew is married to Caroline, a solicitor. They have two young sons, Josiah and Jacob.

Contents

Foreword

In this beautiful but sad book, Canon Andrew White tenderly narrates the story of the suffering and dignity of the people of Iraq caught up in a nightmare of pain and agony beyond our understanding. As I read Andrew's moving and observant account I was taken back to my late teens when I was in the Royal Air Force and served for fifteen months at RAF Shaibah, near Basra. I too got to know the Iraqis and found them to be an intelligent, advanced and caring people. It was there I was first introduced to Islam and began to appreciate its significance in our world. Canon White brings this different culture to light as he introduces us to people like Fatima who lost all her nine children during allied bombing in 1991 and Ahmed and Immanuel whose maimed bodies bear the scars of the same conflict.

Andrew, of course, is well equipped to tell this story because he knows the Middle East well and has an amazing track record of faith in action and of Christian compassion that moves beyond words and slogans into political engagement.

At the time of writing it is still uncertain whether the United States, Britain and their allies are going to invade Iraq to bring Saddam Hussein to judgment. Whatever the future, we are going to need Christian leaders like Andrew White and the Coventry Centre for Reconciliation that he represents, to show to the Iraqi people that the crucified Lord does make all things new and offers a better future.

Lord George Carey
formerly 103rd Archbishop of Canterbury

Introduction

This little book is an unfinished story of an encounter with the people and nation of Iraq. It is the story of a journey backwards and forwards across a long desert road in an attempt to build bridges of reconciliation. It is the story of a personal struggle to engage the reconciling message of the Cross in a nation full of conflict and ambiguities.

This message has been at the heart of the community of Coventry Cathedral since it was bombed at the beginning of World War II. Since that day in 1940, Coventry Cathedral has developed a world-wide community dedicated to reconciliation, known as the Community of the Cross of Nails. The Community, along with the International Centre for Reconciliation, has been at the forefront of the churches' ministry of reconciliation.

This account was written in the safety and tranquillity of Clare College Cambridge as talk of pending war with Iraq filled the headlines of our media. It is not the full story, which cannot yet be told as it may put people in grave danger.

It is not the full story also because part of it is still too awful to tell. One day, maybe I will find the strength to tell the story as I have heard and seen it. But until then, I offer you this encounter.

Though this book is not full of great spiritual wisdom, I hope that it will enable you to gain a little insight into the beauty of the people of Iraq and the terrible situation in which they live. I hope that it may help you discern the will of God and that you may be able to pray more effectively for the nation and people of Iraq.

Chapter 1

The Long Road to Babylon

In 1998 the world was just beginning to wake up to the extent of suffering of the Iraqi people. Eight years of sanctions had a devastating effect on the whole nation. Stories were beginning to filter through of increased infant mortality, starving children and a seriously crumbling infrastructure. One in eight children were dying by the age of five, over six million Iraqis officially malnourished, and the whole nation declared a public health disaster. In addition, there were disturbing stories of the residual effects of depleted uranium (DU) used as a weapon covering in order to aid missile penetration.

Gathering first-hand information of what was really going on proved to be nearly impossible. What was known, however, was the fact that over 400,000 sorties had been flown since the end of the Gulf War. There were stories of innocent people being killed in the areas of the US/British-declared "no-fly zone." Instigated at the end of the war in order to protect minorities in the North and the South, there was evidence here that the regime of Saddam had massacred thousands with chemical weapons.

Much of the information that had been made available to the world had come from the former UN humanitarian

Co-ordinator for Iraq, Denis Haliday. Denis, an Irish Quaker, had resigned from his post on the grounds that the UN Sanctions system was immoral and the cause of great suffering to the Iraqi people. He had been replaced by a serious senior UN diplomat of thirty years' standing, Count Hans von Sponeck.

It was obvious that if Coventry's International Centre for Reconciliation was to be able to seriously engage in the developing Iraqi crisis, I would personally need to visit. This assumption proved a lot more difficult than it sounded. In 1998 people on the whole did not visit Iraq. It was a remote, distant land, only accessible by road from Jordan. There were very few if any journalists present, and even if you were prepared to make the gruelling journey you could only enter the country with an official invitation from the Government of Iraq.

Even though the UK and Iraq ceased to have diplomatic relations with each other in 1990 an Iraqi Interest Section continues to function out of the Jordanian Embassy. This was the obvious place for me to start to try and gain permission to enter this forgotten land.

My initial enquires bore little fruit. First I was asked, "Why do you want to come to Iraq?" I replied that I was coming from a church organisation committed to reconciliation. We were aware of the plight of the Iraqi people and we wanted to know how we could best help. I was dealt with very abruptly and informed that the Iraqi people did not need our help and that all that they needed was for sanctions to be lifted. It was obvious that the diplomatic route was not going to work.

Soon after I arrived at the Cathedral, I was made aware of the role that Coventry had played in supporting the families of hostages during the Gulf War. This work was under the direction of Stephen and Jose Brooks, two Coventry people who had had friends held captive during the war in Iraq and Kuwait. Not prepared to sit back and do nothing, they established the Gulf Support Group, a telephone service that provided help and support to any who had friends and family caught up in these terrible conflicts.

The Brooks were very much encouraged by the Provost of Coventry, the Very Reverend John Petty. John, a deeply devout man of prayer, got the whole cathedral community behind this project, holding regular prayer vigils in the Chapel of Unity and making space available to those involved in running the support group.

After the war and the return of the hostages, Stephen and Jose Brooks did not give up their tireless efforts to help. They regularly visited Kuwait, working hard to provide holistic help to those who had been so negatively affected by the Gulf War. Stephen was eventually awarded the MBE for his service to the Gulf War Support Group.

In the spirit of Coventry, Jose and Stephen were not just concerned about those who had suffered at the hands of Iraq. Their attention was increasingly being drawn to the plight of the people of Iraq. Having read of our concern in the newspaper they came to see me to explore how we might be able to work together in our efforts to help the people of Iraq. Some of their contacts were very useful, but still we struggled to find the right means to gain an invitation to visit Iraq.

In December of 1998, relationships between the American-British Coalition and Iraq deteriorated rapidly after weapons inspectors reported they were being hindered in their activities. Serious air attacks took place, not just in the no-fly zones but also in Baghdad. Suddenly it seemed more urgent than ever to visit this increasingly isolated country.

Eventually our team decided to pray that God would open doors. In those days the team was still very small, consisting only of Lynn and Karl Fulton-Griffiths, our secretary Muriel Stubbins, and me. Yet it was soon after these prayers that Stephen Brooks contacted me to inform me about an organisation committed to building links with Iraq. This group, called "Friendship Across Frontiers," was led by a British Iraqi called Riad. Within hours of talking to Riad I had received an invitation from Tariq Aziz to visit Baghdad. I was to be expected in Baghdad the following week.

There were practical arrangements that needed to be made quickly. First, there was the issue of needing a new passport. My existing passport was full of Israeli stamps, which would make it impossible to be used for entry to Iraq. After explaining this small problem to the UK Passport Authority, a new one was promptly issued. Then there was the matter of informing the Foreign Office, which as might be imagined, was not very enthusiastic about me visiting the country at all. A compromise was reached, however, and I agreed to first visit the British Embassy in Amman, Jordan to receive a briefing.

I eventually flew to Amman where I was to stay for a day before beginning the long journey to Baghdad. As instructed, I promptly reported to the British Embassy where I received a full briefing on the situation in Iraq. It was admitted that much of this information might have been out of date as it had not been possible for anybody from the Embassy to visit Baghdad for many months.

Also on this agenda was the issue of the two Anglican Churches in Iraq which had been vacated at the time of the Gulf War. There was now very real concern about their state. I had already discussed this matter with Bishop Clive Handford, Bishop of Cyprus and the Gulf, under whom jurisdiction for Iraq fell. He was of course very concerned, not least because he himself had been the rector of St George's Church Baghdad for a short time in 1967. His tenure had been swiftly brought to an end during the Six Day War.

At 4.30 am on Friday 12 March I departed from the Intercontinental Hotel Amman. Riad had by now joined me and there was a real sense of uncertainty as we drove through the dark streets of Amman. The first call to prayer could be heard through the cool morning air as we drove towards the desert road.

Once we approached the desert road, we were suddenly faced with an almost continual train of decrepit-looking oil tankers. This, I soon discovered, was the supply of free oil that Iraq provided for Jordan in return for them allowing access to Iraq via the long desert road. In essence Jordan had become the umbilical cord to this ailing nation.

We stopped at the last oasis before leaving Jordan. There were several shops, more like small warehouses than the grocers' stores they were meant to be. This was where the seasoned travellers of this long desert road stocked up on supplies before entering the supposed barren land of Iraq. Here I purchased bottled water, sweets, toiletries and basic food supplies that I hoped to be able to give to those in need.

Jordan seemed a rather sad place. The late King Hussein had recently died and the nation was still in mourning. Every picture of the King – and there were many – was surrounded by black ribbons, and the people were openly lamenting the loss of their much beloved leader.

Chapter 2

Arrival in Baghdad

The first sign that we were arriving in Iraq was huge pictures of President Saddam Hussein. As we paid our departure tax at the Jordanian border, the imposing pictures were facing us. There was Saddam as the military commander, Saddam with a child on his knee and Saddam looking every bit of an English gentleman out for a day's shooting in the country. We were shown into the smoke-filled VIP lounge. One whole wall was filled with a picture of the president and there appeared to be nothing VIP about this saloon.

A visit to the toilets left me feeling positively nauseous, and it was quite clear that such little rooms now needed to be avoided as much as possible. The VIP suite also had a duty-free display containing a frying pan and an electric kettle. Both items were on sale in US dollars at highly exaggerated prices. Over the years I was to gaze at these pathetic items on many occasions, wondering whether anybody would ever feel the need to purchase them.

The bureaucracy seemed to last forever, but in reality it was only about two hours. Eventually my passport was returned with the familiar request for *baksheesh*. After handing over a few dollars, which I later learnt was two months' wages, we departed for Baghdad.

The road now was far superior to those on the Jordanian side: three lanes wide and very straight. With no fear of speed restrictions, we were soon driving at 170 kilometres per hour through an arid landscape. The road was almost empty, with just the odd oil tanker driving slowly through the desert to its Jordanian destination. Hour after hour we drove at the same speed through the same uninspiring landscape, its monotony only broken by the odd camel or flock of emaciated-looking sheep. By now the heat was penetrating but I was informed that this was cool weather by Iraqi standards.

After several hours of driving, we eventually came to the first change in the landscape, the river Euphrates. We stopped on the bridge and looked over to the rather murky-looking but substantial river. Here was one of the great rivers of Babylon which for thousands of years has been at the centre of ancient civilization.

We continued to drive for another hour before reaching the outskirts of Baghdad. Suddenly we were in the midst of a dirty, hot city, once again surrounded by pictures, mosaics and statues of Saddam. On the surface things looked fairly normal, with substantial modern looking buildings built with attractive yellow oriental bricks. There were lots of cars, particularly orange and white taxis.

Closer inspection revealed that almost all the cars had broken windscreens and many had no windscreens at all. My driver explained that this was the result of sanctions. Car parts could not be imported, thus people just had to make do with what they had. It was now big business in Iraq to try to salvage any useable part from scrapped cars.

As we drove up to the Al Rasheed Hotel, it was immediately familiar from CNN filming of the Gulf War. At one time it had been the best hotel in Baghdad, but now it looked in a fairly sorry state. As I entered the hotel, for the first time since entering Iraq I saw a picture of somebody other than Saddam Hussein.

It was a fine mosaic of George Bush on the floor. Everyone entering the only hotel for international guests in Iraq had to walk over his face. In Middle Eastern culture, this is seen as one of the greatest insults to anyone. Underneath the picture, written in English and Arabic, were the words *BUSH IS CRIMINAL*.

The hotel was full of staff, most of them doing virtually nothing. There was a man who walked up and down the lobby all day, every day, cleaning the floor. There was a man who stood next to each lift, who would spend the day cleaning the tarnished brass and press the button for you when you entered. Then there were the many staff at reception who gave me forms to fill out, and then more forms.

At length I was given my keys and told that I was a guest of the foreign ministry. They would pay for my accommodation and food – I was handed a small paper card to produce every time I used the restaurant – but I would have to pay for my telephone bill. Little did I realise at that time that making a telephone call in Iraq was near impossible, let alone trying to call outside the country.

I was then met by Jabber, the man from the protocol department. He informed me that he would be with me throughout my stay, would do anything he could for me and also be my translator. He assured me that there was a very good car – a Mercedes – at my constant disposal, twenty-four hours a day.

Eventually I left for my room, stopping at the washroom on my way. There was a man to open the door. Inside there was another man to turn on the taps, and after I washed my hands, he passed me some toilet tissue to dry my hands on. It then became obvious that this service was not gratis: they needed a tip. Not yet having any Iraqi dinars, I handed them a dollar each.

My room was clean and large. The sheets on the bed were grey – not dirty, just well used. The air conditioning did not work; neither did any of the other appliances in the room apart from one channel on the television that seemed to be showing constant pictures of the great president caring for his people.

After I had unpacked there was a knock at the door: "Please Mr Andrew, we need you to change rooms." I did not argue but packed and moved to a room two floors up. The room was identical but this time there was a man sitting outside the room. I got to know him quite well in the days that I was one of his guests. Every time I left my room he would stand, nod his head and put a tick in his small scrap of paper. Each time I returned he would do the same.

Riad, who had accompanied me from Amman, was not staying at the hotel with me but with some friends in the centre of the city. That night I was to have dinner with the family. Rose and Sami were delightful people, Chilean Christians living as an extended family in a large single-storey home. The family were obviously middle class and had previously enjoyed a very high standard of living. Now, however, they faced the same fate as the majority of the nation, only limited income, rationing of supplies, no future and very temperamental electricity supply.

As we sat in near darkness with only the light of a solitary candle, the family spoke of their fear. "It's the bombs that I'm so scared of," said one of the daughters-in-law. "Last month they were landing very close to our home." The family went on to tell stories of the immense suffering of those who lived around them who were not as fortunate as them.

There were stories of ten or more people living in one

room with no food, apart from meagre rations. Stories of the children were the most distressing. Could it really be true that there was such a high incidence of paediatric malignancies, malnutrition and congenital deformities? In the following days all of my worst fears were to be confirmed.

At the end of the evening I went to change money. The Iraqi dinar had been a very strong currency; each had been worth three US dollars until the Gulf War. Now there were well over 2,000 dinars to the dollar. For the two hundred dollar bills I exchanged, I was presented with a black sack full of notes weighing several kilos. Not surprisingly, most people in any position of importance carried around a case of cash.

On the way back to the Hotel we stopped at the Anglican church of St George of Mesopotamia. It was seriously dilapidated. The windows and pews had all been stolen. Nothing was left apart from the shell.

The Iraqi lawyer representing the church had recently appointed a caretaker named Hanna who was living with his wife in the dilapidated church hall. Our visit with Hanna was good. He had never met anybody from the Church of England and I had to make clear to him that I was not his boss; he worked for Bishop Clive who was based in Cyprus. I assured him that his bishop would soon come.

Over the following months I would spend many hours with Hanna. He did not know what his job really was. For thirteen years he had been a prisoner of war in Iran, most of the time with his hands chained together. He had been held in a remote mountain location, and his release had only happened a few months previously. He had already married Rhema and she was expecting their first child.

The following morning I was to run into my first problem in the hotel. I had stupidly turned up for breakfast without the small identification card. I showed my keys and informed the staff of my room number. This was obviously not going to work. How on earth was I going to be fed without my card? I returned fifteen minutes later with the required card, which was then scrutinised for a further fifteen minutes before I was allowed my morning meal of a shrivelled egg, dry bread and even drier salad. It was a mistake I was never to make again.

Jabber was waiting for me as I left the restaurant. The first stop of the day was the Amira Air Raid Shelter. Although I have seen some horrific scenes, I was not prepared for what I was about to encounter.

The shelter was very substantial, made of several metres' thick concrete reinforced with steel; the door alone weighed over three tonnes. On the night of the 14 February 1991, towards the end of the Gulf War, the shelter had received a direct hit. Right through the middle was a hole through which the missile had penetrated like a knife through a piece of cheese. The sun shone through the shaft amongst the rubble and distorted steel girders. A bird flew in and out singing brightly but all around was the stench of death.

Those who had been killed in the shelter that early morning seven years ago were mainly women and children. All around the walls were pictures of those who had died: Muslims and Christians burnt to death together. In one corner there was a small altar with a cross and candlesticks, an attempt by some of the Christian relatives to bring a little of heaven into this living hell.

The whole scene was reminiscent of the many death camps I have visited in Eastern Europe where Jews were slaughtered in their millions. But the worst image was still to come. Fatima pointed amongst the carnage where a perfect silhouette of a mother holding her child was blasted onto the wall. Near to this imprint were others of people who in their death had become a permanent emblem of the cost of war.

As I saw the imprint of the mother and child it was fixed permanently in my own mind. At the talk of war, it is always this terrible image that is fixed in my mind. As we moved on, Fatima pointed again, this time to a collection of nine pictures of children, from early teens to a young baby. "These are my children," she stated quietly in Arabic. "Your children?" I responded "in unbelief".

I was then told the story of how awful the bombing had been that day. Fatima had taken all of her children to the shelter for protection. After many hours her children were getting hungry so she risked going home to prepare food for the family. As she left her home to return to the shelter the bomb struck. All of her children were killed.

As I departed, I was asked to sign the visitor's book. What do you write in the midst of such devastation? I simply wrote the words, "May the souls of these faithful children rest in peace and rise in glory. Father, forgive."

I handed Fatima a few small gifts and assured her of my prayers. She then looked at the cross of nails hanging around my neck and kissed it. I was surprised at this action as the lady was obviously a devout Muslim. She seemed transfixed by this cross.

Through Jabber asked her if she would like one, to which she responded with an eager smile. I went to the car and brought her two crosses, a free-standing brass Cross of Nails and a small necklace. As I gave her these gifts I told her the story of Coventry and gave her a copy of the litany of reconciliation.

I have visited this shelter many times since that first awful visit; the experience never gets any easier. To this day, the Cross of Nails and litany of reconciliation are still on the altar there.

Each visitor I have brought to Iraq over the years has been taken to the shelter – it is an expected part of the programme. Some say this is part of Iraqi propaganda, and maybe it is. But to the world it is also an unforgettable reminder of the futility and danger of war.

The Gulf War was seen by the world as we watched the images on CNN. To many it was the first "clean war," as laser-guided missiles were directed to targets with pin-point precision. But on the ground it was very different. As with all wars, it is real people who die, women and children, defenceless innocents caught in the evil web of the sinfulness of humanity.

From the shelter we travelled to the Saddam Children's Hospital. The building was modern, only about fifteen years old, but in a severe state of disrepair. I was shown into the office of the medical director. He gave me in-depth statistics of the kind of cases they now had to deal with: pneumonia in the winter, and cholera and typhoid in the summer. The latter two illnesses were almost unheard of in Iraq before the Gulf War.

As the medical director chain-smoked his cigarettes, he went on to explain the huge increase in the incidence of childhood leukaemia and other malignancies. It was thought that much of this new pathology was the result of depleted uranium (DU) used in the missiles of the Gulf War and the continued bombing that was taking place in the north and south of the country. Then he spoke of the malnutrition, and the rapidly increasing infant mortality rate. The statistics were horrifying.

Finally I visited the wards, where there was no noise: no sound of children playing or even crying. There were very few obvious members of staff, but bed after bed of emaciated children, yellow in complexion, most with no hair. Parents sat next to their children, many with tears streaming down their face as they watched their little loved ones dying.

Dr Al Ghabban, a young oncology registrar, talked me through each child's case history. Many children had acute myeloid leukaemia; others, lymphatic leukaemia and some sarcoma. It was explained to me that many of these children would have had a very high chance of going into remission if only the right treatment was available. But most medicines, especially cytotoxic drugs were banned under the sanctions regime because they were considered dual-use items. Even simple antibiotics were very difficult to get hold of.

The other major problem was that of complementarity. It might be possible to get one item, but that what was needed to go with it would not be available. So on the day I visited the hospital, drip sets were available but they had run out of the canulas to go into the vein.

I do not think I had ever felt so helpless in face of such need. Many of the children were in great pain but even that could not be helped because adequate analgesia was also not available.

From the hospital I went to see the Minister of Health, Dr Umeed Mubarak. He is a quietly spoken, sophisticated man; a Kurd, dressed in the green uniform of the Revolutionary Guard (Saddam's cabinet). Once again I was presented with statistics of how the health of the nation had seriously deteriorated. By this stage I was eager to know what, if anything, I could do to help. In response, it was quite obvious that the Iraqis wanted me to tell the story of what I had seen.

As I left the Minister's office I was faced with a barrage of reporters and TV cameras. The questions came thick and fast. "What do you think of sanctions? What will you be telling your government? What did you see in the hospital? Do you condemn sanctions?"

These questions all represented issues that I had to suddenly face head on. I had now seen a little with my own eyes of what was happening. I now had a huge responsibility. How would I respond?

Over the next few days I continued to have a broad range of meetings. For most of them I was accompanied by Jabbal, my minder. I was growing rather fond of him. He was a very quiet man and despite the fact he was working for Iraqi intelligence, he was good company.

I did however manage to have a considerable time away from my translator, Ziad, when Sami, the man I had met on my first night, took me to various Christian institutions. It was on one such visit that I went to the Mother Theresa home of the Sisters of Charity in Baghdad.

Mother Theresa had visited Iraq after the Gulf War in 1993. She had been shocked by what was beginning to happen to the children. She left three of her sisters to establish a new work of caring for unwanted children.

This community was to become a place of almost regular pilgrimage. Within the walls of this house was a different world. This world was still affected by the suffering outside but redeemed by love, the love of four Indian sisters.

Living with the sisters were twenty-five children, all under the age of eight, and all suffering some form of disability. Some of the children had severe learning difficulties while others were only physically disabled. Several children had serious congenital deformities such as Ahmed and Immanuel.

Ahmed and Immanuel are two of the most beautiful little boys I have ever met. They both have no arms or legs, just small stumps for limbs. They are unable to feed themselves but somehow manage to move around the floor. They both speak English with an Indian accent, and never seem happier than when they can entertain guests, especially guests who speak English. They love to be held and cuddled and will always respond by giving you a kiss.

Both boys are very bright. I can remember thinking that one day Ahmed and Immanuel would have to face the outside world when they would realise how different they are. All of these children had been disowned, some just left on the streets. Others had parents who were just too horrified by their appearance and had handed them over. Many, however, came from families who were just too poor to cope with the expense of a disabled child.

I gave all of the children some sweets and small gifts. They then sang me a simple song of thanks followed by "Ave Maria" and some children's choruses. Ahmed and Immanuel were not brothers but they clearly thought they were. With similar disabilities and only a year apart in age they had so much in common. Their final act to impress me was a backward summersault, which would have been impressive for any child, let alone one who had no arms or legs!

Like all of the children I met in Iraq, these children had very little, yet they had the most important thing in life, love. This love was shown to them continually by the four sisters who never had a day off. They never went on holiday, but simply served God by serving his children.

I was not long back at the hotel when Jabbal came to find me. "You must come quickly; Mr Tariq Aziz wants to see you now." I quickly put my cassock on, having been told I must look like a priest, and jumped into the back of the car. The car roared off at high speed, went through red lights and sped down the centre of the road. Other cars just parted and gave way; it was like Moses at the Red Sea.

It was only after several visits that I began to understand this phenomenon which seemed to happen so regularly. I was in a presidential car which could be identified by its number plate. People were giving way out of fear, rather than politeness.

We eventually arrived at the office of the Deputy Prime Minister. There was minimal security and the building was modest compared to the Ministry of Health. After a short wait in the usual smoke-filled waiting room that you find in the Arab world, with its Arabic coffee and blaring television, I was shown into the office of Mr Aziz. Tariq Aziz is a small man in the usual Revolutionary Guard uniform and brown leather slip-on shoes. He nearly always has a very large cigar in his hand which he only rarely seems to smoke.

After the normal welcome and exchange of pleasantries he began to tell me how close the Iraqi people were to the British. He spoke of the time he had spent at Chequers, the country home of British prime ministers, and his relationship with Margaret Thatcher and Geoffrey Howe. "In the good days," he said, "we would come to London and spend the weekend shopping in Harrods."

This theme of the close ties between Britain and Iraq seemed to be genuine and was repeated by almost all of the politicians that I met with. Many of them had come to England for their post-graduate university studies.

After a while we got on to the serious topics: sanctions, weapons inspectors, espionage, depleted uranium and the Gulf War. In the early days of my visits to Iraq it was clear that the Iraqi regime thought that Britain was in the hands of the US administration.

Tariq Aziz had his own clear agenda of what he wanted out of our meeting. My visit was obviously considered to be of importance – after all, at this stage very few people were visiting Iraq. Mr Aziz clearly wanted me to be a regular visitor from the very beginning; there was no notion of this being a one-off.

But I also had an agenda. In addition to wanting to show

real concern for the people of Iraq and wanting to establish what could be done to help end this dreadful suffering, I needed to use this meeting to establish the status of the Anglican Church here.

By now I had already visited the Anglican Church of St George of Mesopotamia, in its unenviable position next door to the Ministry of Information and most of Iraq's satellite information. The church was derelict: everything that could be stolen had been stolen – doors, pews, windows and pulpit. The only thing that remained was the font which was solid marble and had obviously been too heavy to budge. There were a few remaining war memorials to those who had fallen in service especially during the First World War. If this church was to survive it needed help urgently.

I informed Tariq Aziz of the situation and asked him if the Bishop of Cyprus and the Gulf could be permitted to visit. His response was very positive. Not only was this permission granted, but Mr Aziz even suggested that an Anglican priest could return and that the church should be restored.

Having moved to matters ecclesiastical I was then invited to bring a delegation of bishops back with me at the earliest opportunity. After informing him that I would try and see what could be arranged, I promised to return in the not-too-distant future.

The meeting had lasted over an hour and at last I felt that we were making a little headway in trying to help the Iraq people. Just a week earlier I had still been trying to find a way of entering Iraq. I had now had a lightning encounter with this ancient and complex land and had already spent over an hour with the *de facto* Prime Minister.

That night I returned to my hotel with such a mixture of feelings. I was desperately sad and perplexed. I knew that we were now involved in Iraq long term, but what the future would be I just did not know.

That evening I read Psalm 137, a song from the Hebrew exile:

> *"By the rivers of Babylon we sat down and wept*
>   *when we remembered Zion."*

But it was the fourth verse that particularly hit me:

> *"How can we sing the songs of the LORD*
>   *while in a foreign land?"*

Now the people of Babylon are in a strange land in their own country. They who once had so much now have nothing.

My following days in Baghdad were filled with a whole series of meetings with both religious and political leaders. Everybody that I met was gracious and hospitable. But there were two further encounters which were truly memorable.

The first was with the Chaldean Patriarch who is Beatitude Raphael Bidawid I, Patriarch of all Babylon and the Chaldeans. The Chaldeans are the major Christian denomination in Iraq. They are Assyrians who like the Syrian Orthodox pray in the ancient Aramaic language – the language used by Jesus. The Chaldeans are an Eastern right of the Catholic Church and thus come under the authority of the Pope in Rome. The Patriarch was dressed in the scarlet robes of a Cardinal and looked very similar to Pope John XXIII.

He spoke of what had happened to the Christian community; of how the church was trying to provide what help it could to those most in need and the now familiar story of how sanctions had brought a great nation to its knees. I found it difficult, however, when he began blaming the Zionists for the demise of Iraq. One of the people who were accompanying me that day immediately agreed and started adding to the anti-Zionist comments. I bit my lip and said nothing. It was several months before I would really understand what was going on in this meeting.

Another memorable meeting was with the Ayatollah Al Sider, one of Iraq's most respected Shia spiritual leaders. Sitting on the floor in an alcove of the beautiful Al Kadhimia Mosque in the centre of Baghdad, he began by quoting words of the Quran before welcoming us to the mosque. Just as he was about to begin serious conversation, a bride and groom entered the alcove. With little fuss he quickly married them, gave them a blessing and they and their families went on their way rejoicing.

The Ayatollah continued to speak of how important it was for Islam and Christianity to work together. Although he spoke a little of Ali, the founder of Shia Islam, he said nothing which was politically sensitive. He would not enter into conversation about the tensions between Sunni and Shia Muslims or the stories of persecution of the Shia by the regime of Saddam. All of this would be revealed much later and in another place.

That night in the Al Rasheed hotel there was a wonderful pianist playing in the foyer. The whole scene was very reminiscent of an Eastern European hotel in the days of communism.

As I sat thinking through the remarkable events of the day, I was approached by a smiling young lady who introduced herself to me as Mona from the *Baghdad Observer*. The first thing that struck me was her broad Yorkshire accent, not quite what I would have expected from Iraq's only English newspaper. She informed me that she had spent some of her youth in Yorkshire and had been to school in Leeds.

Mona wanted to know if I had been following her stories about me in her newspaper, that is, her government's newspaper. I had to confess that I had not. She handed me a copy. It was quite simply the worst produced paper I had ever seen. The print was almost unreadable and the pictures were undistinguishable, that is, apart from the one of Saddam at the head of the paper which was followed by some of the President's words of wisdom.

We sat and talked, drinking not very nice mint tea. Even things that the Iraqis did well were not very good at the Al Rasheed! Mona wanted to know my life story and what it was that made me care about Iraq. She then went on to tell me about herself, how she loved poetry and art, and did some painting herself, and that it just so happened that her pictures were on sale in one of the shops at the hotel. She took me off to the shop and there propped up against a stuffed tiger's head was her picture, very bright, with child-like simplicity depicting a woman flying on a unicorn over Baghdad.

Mona was also to become a key figure in our engagement with the people of Iraq. But before she departed she requested that I make contact with her father who was ill and staying with family in Leeds. I told her I would be only too happy to oblige.

The following morning, I bumped into a man dressed in tennis kit, who said he had been looking for me. He introduced himself as Hans von Sponeck. I was amazed that now, just moments before departure, I met the one person whom I had not managed to see from my list of people that I felt I must meet.

Count Hans von Sponeck was the Assistant Secretary General of the United Nations, the most senior UN figure who had held the portfolio of UN Humanitarian Co-ordinator for Iraq. It was quite clear from our short meeting that we were on the same wavelength. Hans very much encouraged me to continue the mission I had begun and

assured me of his total support. He expressed his grave
concern over the nature of the sanctions regime which he
was in part responsible for. Von Sponeck was also to become
a very important part of our ongoing work in Iraq.

As I prepared to leave the hotel, my minder Jabber
pleaded with me to try and do something to help his
ill children. One of the saddest experiences of the week
was watching him following me around the children's
hospital, asking physician after physician if they had any
of the drugs that his children needed. After giving Jabbal
my leftover bag of Iraqi dinars and an embrace, I departed
for Amman.

The journey back seemed longer than the one coming. My
mind was full of images, disturbed and bewildered. What
could I do with such an experience? Would anybody listen
to the story and would they believe it? For the first time on
any of my travels I had gone to Iraq with a BBC tape
recorder. Midlands BBC was hoping that they would be able
to use some recordings that I was able to make throughout
the week. In the end I had over seven hours of recording,
which were eventually turned by the BBC into a one-hour
broadcast.

After ten hours I eventually arrived at the world's worst
VIP lounge at the desert border. Crossing the border into
Jordan, I was greatly reassured to see the friendly pictures
of the late King Hussein. A Jordanian policeman greeted
me with a big smile, exclaiming "Welcome to Jordan."
Although in a short time I had become very fond of the
people of Iraq, I was certainly glad to be in Jordan. Knowing
that I was no longer being watched 24 hours a day was a
great relief.

Reporting back to the British Embassy in Amman was
easier than I thought it would be. The diplomatic staff were
clearly very interested in the details of my visit. My initial

assessment of the dangerous nature of the present sanctions regime was also accepted graciously.

On my return to England I was immediately contacted by the press. What had I done? Who had I met? Was it dangerous? Did I feel in danger? There was the sense that I had taken a week's holiday in the lions' den and miraculously had survived! People were honestly surprised when I stressed what a warm reception I had received and how keen I was to return as soon as possible.

On one radio interview I mentioned that Tariq Aziz had invited me to return with my bishop and other Church leaders. A few minutes later I received a call from Colin Bennetts, the Bishop of Coventry, asking when we were going. Bishop Colin has always been at the heart of his Cathedral's ministry of reconciliation. I always know that he is willing to take risks for the sake of reconciliation and would not ask us to do anything that he was not prepared to do himself.

The desk officers at the Foreign and Commonwealth office were nowhere near as courteous as the staff at the Embassy in Amman. I was informed in no uncertain terms that I was being used as propaganda for Saddam's regime and that I had been fooled into believing Iraqi lies.

However, the foreign minister then dealing with Iraq was the MP Derek Fatchet. He himself was very supportive of what we were trying to do and wrote to me on 26 April 1999 stating that *"the report on your earlier visit makes disturbing reading; on the humanitarian side, it reinforces our view that more must be done to address the needs of the Iraqi people."* The relationship with the minister continued to be positive but sadly, a few days before I was due to meet him, he suddenly died. He was replaced by the present Minister of Defence, Geoffrey Hoon.

Meanwhile, plans were continuing for our return visit

with the Episcopal delegation. My report had also been sent
to the Archbishop of Canterbury, George Carey, who invited
me to visit him with the Bishops before we departed for Iraq.
The Archbishop also requested that we include Dr Charles
Reed in the delegation who was the assistant secretary for
international affairs at the Board of Social Responsibility of
the Church of England.

Chapter 3

The First Return to Iraq

After six weeks of discussions and an exchange of letters with the FCO, we were ready to return to Baghdad. The delegation was to consist of the Bishop of Coventry Colin Bennetts, the Bishop of Cyprus and the Gulf Clive Handford, and the then Bishop of Kingston Peter Price. Also joining us was Charles Reed, Patrick Sookhdeo of the Barnabas Fund and Ian Young Archdeacon of Cyprus and the Gulf.

We arrived in Jordan a day before departure in order to have our briefing with Sir Christopher Battiscombe, the British Ambassador. Sir Christopher was the best of the old school of British diplomats, the perfect English gentleman. The briefing meeting went well. Once again there was the request that we inform the Embassy of our findings. We also tried to contact Prince Raad, a member of the Hasmonite Royal Family who is the rightful heir to the Iraqi throne.

After a night in Amman we left for Iraq on 10th May at 4.30 am. This time I knew what to expect and was very much looking forward to my return. All of the delegates had done their homework well. They had studied the statistics and knew the problems that the Iraqi people were suffering. They were all people of great calibre, and despite taking the initiative very seriously, they were also able to enjoy themselves and laugh at themselves and each other.

Our journey to Baghdad was uneventful and we were all welcomed back to the Al Rasheed Hotel like long-lost friends. Jabber was waiting for us along with some of his friends from the Department of Protocol who had come to accompany our delegation – after all, one man could not be expected to watch six men! There were now three Mercedes, all with damaged windscreens and black curtains on the back windows.

Mona was also in the hotel lobby, waiting to greet the delegation in her broad Yorkshire accent. The delegation was clearly amused at such a reception, but it was just the beginning of their Baghdad experience. Despite the fact that the Iraqis had known for several days that we were coming, no meetings had been arranged. The one meeting already in place was with Count Hans von Sponeck, the UN Humanitarian Coordinator. This was possible because the UN did not rely on the Iraq phone system. To talk to their office you phoned not Baghdad but New York.

As we drove into the UN compound it was quite clear that our minders were slightly on edge about this meeting. However, they did not need to fear. Von Sponeck gave an articulate presentation of the devastating effect of sanctions on the people of Iraq. One by one he dispelled the propaganda and myths that were common in the west. These included reports that the Iraqis were stockpiling medicine and food, causing the shortages themselves. He spoke to us of the cumbersome process of having to pass all requests through the 661 committee in New York. This was the committee which was established under the oil for food programme and had to approve every item imported into Iraq. In an attempt to ensure that no item had dual use even lead pencils for school children were banned for several years. Han von Sponeck saw that this process was directly contributing to the suffering of the most vulnerable.

We left the UN feeling depressed but certain that we were on the right mission for this time. The compound had previously also been the base of the weapons inspectors who had recently been expelled by Iraq for supposed involvement in espionage and the looting of ancient Babylonian antiquities.

From the UN base we went to visit the Anglican Church. Bishop Clive was clearly disturbed by what he saw although pleased to be back in a part of his diocese that he had not visited for over thirty years. I was able to introduce Hannah, the new caretaker, to his boss for the first time. We prayed in the church and agreed that we would return for a service on the coming Sunday.

Throughout the week we visited all of the places and people that I had met on my previous visit. The response was predictable. There was the real anguish and pain at the visits to the shelter and the children's hospital, the frustrations of the Al Rasheed Hotel and warm humble hospitality of the Iraqi people. The joy of the visit to the Mother Theresa home was also significant. As we entered there again we saw those two delightful boys Ahmed and Immanuel. I held them tightly, one in each arm. Ahmed said that Immanuel had told him that he knew I would come back.

One of the highlights of the trip was a meeting with Hermez Hannah, another Chaldean Christian. Hermez had visited Bishop Colin's parish when he was vicar of St Andrew's Church in Oxford. His son worshipped at the church and Bishop Colin had baptised their children.

Hermez invited us to visit him at his home in Dora, one of the large towns within Baghdad on the following Saturday. We visited his church, St John the Baptist, a large modern building in need of much repair like most Iraqi buildings.

Then the priest, Father Maher, brought out their prize possession. It was a chalice given to the church several years ago by Bishop Colin and his Oxford parish. It was strange for me to see Bishop Colin being shown such great respect, not for being a senior bishop of the Church of England, but because once he had been the vicar of St Andrews, North Oxford.

Hermez's wife Maria then presented us with what was probably the finest meal I have ever experienced in my years of travel. The main dish was *masgouf*, a very large fish from the Tigris weighing at least fifteen kilos and cooked on an open fire. Our ever-present minders seemed to appreciate the meal as much as we did. The time, cost and love that had gone into its production were quite phenomenal.

After lunch we tried desperately hard to talk to the family without our friends from the Ministry. Eventually we went for a walk in the family's small vegetable patch and for the first time with this delegation were able to hear something of the real dilemmas of the Iraqi people. These dilemmas are so complex and so frightening that the full story cannot yet be told. One day, maybe very soon, that day will come.

Our programme nearly complete, we returned to the Al Rasheed. All that remained was the meeting with Tariq Aziz. Not knowing when this meeting would happen, we began to hope that it would be that night, Saturday.

As we entered the hotel lobby we were informed that there were people waiting to see us. Sitting in the centre of the lobby was a very large Egyptian man, obviously not suffering the effects of sanctions. He was the pastor of the main evangelical Church in Baghdad and clothed in a traditional Protestant Geneva preaching gown. Not something which is usually worn out of the pulpit.

Accompanying him was another man of slight stature, dressed smartly in a suit. He introduced himself to me as

Georges Sada, the President of the Protestant Churches in Iraq. Georges and his friend had been informed by the ministry of Al Qaf (Religious Affairs) that we were in town and had come to greet us. This low key, almost incidental meeting was to prove to be the most significant of all our meetings in Iraq, perhaps a divine appointment, for Georges would soon become our man in Baghdad.

Shortly after this meeting we were informed that tonight was the night we would meet the deputy Prime Minister, Tariq Aziz. We were all relieved that this meeting would actually happen, as the bishops had issues they wanted to discuss in the light of all that we had seen. As in all of our formal meetings we dressed in our cassocks and made our way to our waiting convoy of cars. A chase through the night streets brought us to Aziz's dilapidated offices.

Tariq Aziz received us like long-lost friends; he was delighted that I had been able to return so soon with such a senior delegation. It was probably at this moment that he decided that it was worth investing in our relationship. From this day I was always able to see him, in fact in the months and years to come I would be invited to see him on every visit, even when I had no particular need to engage with him.

The conversation followed the now familiar pattern, dealing in turn with the problems of sanctions, the Iraqis' love of the British, and what needed to be done to help Iraq. Towards the end of this dialogue Mr Aziz came up with a suggestion that we immediately thought was worth pursuing. He proposed that we should invite the religious leaders of Iraq to visit the UK and the USA. The UK part of this plan sounded easy enough; with the backing of the Archbishop of Canterbury we were sure we could get them into the UK.

The USA would be rather more difficult. At this point, Tariq Aziz made a passing statement which was to be absolutely true. He told us that probably the only person who could pull this event off in the US was Billy Graham. We left assuring the deputy Prime Minister that we would certainly try and bring the project to fruition.

The following morning we were due to depart for Amman but before we did so we had arranged to have a service of Holy Communion in the Anglican Church. We had informed all of the Christians that we had met that we would be having this service and lo and behold, Count Hans von Sponeck was there with several of his staff, Hermez and Maria and their family had come, as had Georges Sada and the whole of Hanna the caretaker's extended family.

By now Hanna had made a great effort to clean up the church and clear out the evidence of the scores of pigeons that had taken refuge there. He had also done his best to make the church look like church as he knew it. There was a poster of Mary, the brass Coventry Cross of Nails on the altar and burning incense. Not exactly what you would expect in an Anglican church, but all of Hanna's efforts were deeply moving and appreciated.

We all took part in this simple service of Holy Communion in a broken church in a broken land. We sang, prayed, celebrated Holy Communion, shared the peace and experienced an overwhelming presence of the Holy Spirit in our midst. There are not words to describe what happened in that service but we were on holy ground and the glory of the Lord moved through that place. Over the following years I would learn how significant the service had been for all who were present.

After the service we went into the dilapidated church hall which was also the home of Hanna and his wife Rema. There we were served with Arab coffee and in this most humble of surroundings shown great love, which by now we knew was a trait of so many of the Iraqi people.

As we prepared to depart Georges Sada came to us and

assured us that he would do whatever he could to aid us in our mission. He also promised to help keep an eye on the church and make sure that Hanna and his family were well looked after. Georges was a man of his word, and since that day has taken care of our every need in our ongoing work in Iraq. The whole congregation gathered as we entered the large vehicles which were to take us back to Amman.

As we drove back across that long desert road, once again we were filled with mixed emotions. We had entered a hidden world ruled over by the iron rod of Saddam, and yet had had the privilege of meeting something beautiful and simple.

We also felt some responsibility for the dreadful calamity that had come over this ancient land of the Tigris and Euphrates. This broken people, in a broken land are part of a broken world. As we once again crossed these two great rivers, a modern rendition of Psalm 137 again rang through my ears: *"By the rivers of Babylon where we sat down, there we wept when we remembered Zion."*

As we entered Jordan and a mobile phone signal returned, I phoned Prince Raad to see if there was any chance that we could meet up. He said that he would be delighted to meet us and that he would send cars to take us to the palace once we were back in Amman.

We eventually arrived back at our hotel in Amman at about 8 pm that night. We were all rather tired, and in need of refreshment and exercise. Most of the delegation headed for the swimming pool while I continued to make arrangements with Prince Raad. Suddenly there was an urgent call to go to the hotel reception: there was a message from the Prince. Knowing how tired we must all be, he had decided to come to the hotel rather than expect us to visit him. He would arrive in ten minutes.

I had only a few minutes to round up our group of bishops

from the pool and sauna to prepare them for our meeting with the Prince, who arrived within the allotted time. The hotel management was obviously impressed and started to ask questions about who exactly we were. The Prince said he would like to stay for dinner and we were given the best table in a quiet location.

Bishop Colin began by sending condolences to the royal family on the death of the much beloved King Hossain. We went on to discuss all that we had seen and experienced in Iraq. The Prince repeated several times what a desperate tragedy the whole situation was. It was only then that we discovered that he is in fact the rightful heir to the Iraqi throne.

Due to lack of time we never had the opportunity to report back to the Embassy but as we entered the plane, there was Sir Christopher Battiscombe, the British Ambassador. Throughout the flight we were able to discuss with him what we had witnessed. When we came to the issue of Hans von Sponeck we were informed that some within the Foreign and Commonwealth Office thought von Sponeck had "gone native," meaning specifically that he was adopting Iraqi ideology. We were all rather shocked by this perception. Von Sponeck was a much-respected UN diplomat, having given a lifetime of service, and quite clearly a man of great integrity. This passing remark was to foreshadow much of what we were to face in our dealings with our Foreign Office in the coming months.

Back in the UK I was surprised that there was less interest from the media about this visit than my previous solitary one. Reports were prepared for the FCO and the Archbishop of Canterbury, while letters were exchanged between ministers and ourselves. The general line was that Her Majesty's Government was very concerned about the Iraqi people but Saddam needed to be contained.

Chapter 4

From Babylon to the Big Apple

We were now faced with a substantial challenge. How could we get these Iraqi religious leaders to Britain and the US in the next two or three months? It was clear from the beginning that we had the backing of both the Archbishop of Canterbury and the Foreign Office. The British side of the programme would not be too difficult. It was simply the matter of finding the money and organising the programme. As regards the US part of the trip that was another matter.

My starting point was to try and track down Dr Billy Graham. The former leader of Coventry Cathedral's Community of the Cross of Nails in the USA is a retired professor named Van Kussrow. He lives in Hendersonville, North Carolina, which just happens to be Billy Graham country. I phoned Van and explained to him the situation and what we needed to achieve in a very short space of time.

Within an hour he had tracked down the precise person that I needed to speak with: Dr John Ackers, Dr Graham's special assistant, who looked after most of his complicated international initiatives. From my first conversation with John Ackers it was quite clear that he was the kind of man I could work with. It just so happened that Dr Graham himself had already expressed his concern over what was happening to the people of Iraq.

John Ackers was certain that Dr Graham would want to be part of such an initiative but assured me that he would discuss the whole idea in full with him and get back to me the next day. The following day's telephone conversation confirmed that Dr Graham was very committed to this whole project. The Billy Graham Association would also fund their round trip from Iraq to New York and home via London. This was another major hurdle that we had jumped.

By now a new head of the Iraqi interest section had arrived in London. It was Dr Mudhafa Amin, a historian who had spent most of his working life in academia, teaching at Baghdad University. He is a very pleasant and gentle man who is also quite an Anglophile, having studied for his PhD at the University of Durham. Dr Amin became my main means of communicating with Baghdad. At this stage communication with Iraq was still near impossible, and I would often spend several hours trying to make one phone call. Even for Dr Amin there was no quick route of communication. Every message had to be sent via the Iraqi Embassy in Paris, from which there would be regular despatches to Baghdad.

After several weeks and another return visit to Iraq I was eventually given the names of the delegation. It was to consist of three key individuals chosen by the government of Iraq to represent their interests. One was to be the Chaldean Patriarch, Raphael Bidawid I. Having now met him on several occasions I was pleased, because he was quite clearly the leading Christian in Iraq. Though not in his first youth, he managed his 70-plus years very well.

The Shia leader would be the kind and gentle Ayatollah Al Sider with whom I had also had a positive encounter. The third member of the delegation and the most influential in the group was not known to me. It was to be Sheik Abdul Latif Humayeem, a senior Sunni leader, president of the Islamic bank of Iraq, a well-known preacher and a close confidant of the president Saddam Hussein.

There was much interest in the proposed visit both in the UK and US. As soon as news got out, invitations started to arrive. If we were to fulfil all these requests, the delegation would need to spend several months out of Iraq. We therefore selected carefully the best opportunities for the team to gain the greatest amount of exposure to both political and religious leaders.

A similar programme was to be arranged in both the US and the UK. Dr John Ackers was also working hard to get the delegates maximum exposure. It was agreed that in the UK their official host would be the Archbishop of Canterbury and in the States Dr Billy Graham.

The American part of the programme was scheduled to last for six days in September 1999. The delegates were to be based for the first part of their programme in New York. Dr Graham was at that time preparing for a major speech there and for a sermon at Harvard the following weekend.

With all the arrangements now made and the assurance that visas would be issued in Amman from both the US and British embassies, I flew to New York on Tuesday 12 September. I arrived at 3 pm and the Iraqi delegation was due in at 7.30 pm. They were to be met by colleagues of Franklin Graham, the son of Dr Billy Graham. Franklin heads up the Christian humanitarian branch of the Billy Graham Association's work known as Samaritan's Purse. Through their contact in Lebanon they had been taking humanitarian supplies into Iraq for several years and were very keen to be involved in the programme.

Dr John Ackers met me at the JFK Airport and accompanied me into the centre of New York where I had been booked into a hotel in Time Square. As we travelled I was made aware of the concern that there was in certain circles about our joint venture. On arrival in New York we talked further and discussed the CIA reports that had been given to us on the delegates.

There was nothing in the report that I did not know already though there were several factual errors. One such error concerned the report of the killing of one of the relatives of the Ayatollah just a month previous. The report stated that it was a distant relative while in fact it was one of his very close relations. Ironically, the report referred to Sheik Abdul Latif Humayeem as the "Billy Graham of Iraq," with particular reference to the popularity of the sheik's Friday sermons on Iraqi television.

As we sat down at dinner we waited anxiously for the telephone call from the airport to inform us of the delegation's arrival into Newark Airport. No confirmation arrived. Just before midnight we were informed that the plane from Jordan had arrived but our delegates had not. We decided that there was nothing that we could do at this late hour and retired for the night.

The next morning we were beginning to get quite anxious, not least because a full itinerary had been arranged and their first meeting was to have been this morning with Dr Graham himself. One of the most frustrating things was having no idea what was going on or what had happened. I phoned the British Embassy in Amman who confirmed that two days previously all the delegates had been issued with their visas to enter the UK. Such information was not forthcoming from the US Embassy who refused to pass any information on to us about their whereabouts. The only remaining solution was to see if my main contact in Jordan could trace our Iraqi delegates.

In the meantime I went over to see Dr Graham in the

Marriott hotel just across the road from where I was staying in Time Square. The meeting was truly memorable. For over three hours we talked about Iraq, mission, evangelism, the Church of England and much more. I was acutely aware that I was sitting in the presence of a holy man. He spoke with such humility and obviously had very little confidence in his own ability. Immediately it was obvious to me why he is often referred to as the "Protestant Pope."

Eventually we had a message from our man in Amman. He had found the delegates in a hotel but they were still being interviewed by the US Embassy. There was no guarantee of when they would be able to leave for the US, but they hoped it could be on the next plane. In the meantime I was in the unenviable position of having to go to the prearranged meetings. Speaking on behalf of the suffering people of Iraq was something that I was becoming quite accustomed to but by now I was deeply frustrated at the lack of progress we were making. I spoke at several meetings where I was able to tell the story from my limited experience. We eventually heard news that our delegates still had not been issued visas and that they had not been able to board today's plane.

In further discussion with Dr Graham it was clear that he would need to take some action. One of the people the delegation was due to meet was former President Jimmy Carter, and it was suggested that he might be able to intervene. Eventually it was decided not to go down this route as the relationship between President Clinton and Carter was somewhat strained at that point.

Eventually Dr Ackers suggested that Dr Graham phone the White House and speak to the President himself. Dr Graham was clear that he would rather leave things, however, because "the President is morally compromised at the moment." It was at the time of the Monica Lewinsky affair and Billy Graham was acutely aware of his own role as the moral conscience of the nation.

By Friday morning we were beginning to become very concerned indeed about the possibility that the delegation might not be granted entry into the US. After the appropriate level of intervention we were finally informed that the delegates had been allowed to board the plane and would arrive in New York on Friday night. By now we had flown to Boston in preparation for Billy Graham's major commitment in Harvard over the weekend.

It was not a good time to be in the Boston area. It was the weekend of the Ryder Cup and every hotel was full to overflowing. It had been impossible for me to find a room in Boston so a hotel room had been booked for me in Cambridge, the home of Harvard University, just a few miles down the road. My room was decent, but not over-lavish, however I was horrified when I discovered that it cost over $750 per night, excluding breakfast. The prices had all been inflated because of the Ryder Cup. How could I stay in a hotel whilst trying to help Iraq, when one night's accommodation cost a lifetime's salary of the average Iraqi worker?

First thing the following morning I went about trying to find a cheaper room, although all of the agencies informed me that there wasn't a room left in town. Suddenly the man I was talking to noticed my clerical collar. "Well," he said, "if you're a man of God it may be another matter." He immediately phoned a monastery around the corner and told them the plight of this poor priest from England. The monastery just happened to be Anglican and belonged to the Cowley Fathers. Although their guest house was closed they were willing for me to stay full board at the cost of $30 a night. I suddenly felt justified in my decision to change accommodation.

While in Cambridge I managed to meet up with a group of

young people from an organisation called "Voices in the Wilderness." I had met them one evening in Baghdad at the Iraqi Airways Office, which was now providing basic business services, Iraqi Airways having not flown for over a decade. International calls there were expensive but nowhere near as costly as the hotel, where they would be in the region of $45. At neither place would you have any guarantee of actually getting through but they would take your money anyway! On the night in question I happened to hear the rare sound of a group of young people speaking in English, so had gone over and introduced myself. Though our missions had a very different approach, we had the same end aim of trying to help the Iraqi people.

We met on several occasions in Iraq, and were delighted to be able to meet up again in their home town of Cambridge. They were very surprised that Billy Graham would be involved in such a venture. I was able to explain that for many years Dr Graham had been involved in quiet behind-the-scenes diplomatic efforts, not least with North Korea and China.

Late Friday night I had a call from John Ackers informing me that our Iraqi delegates had arrived into New York. They were to be met by an Arab-American friend of Franklin Graham who would be flying them in his private plane to his family ranch just outside Boston. We would meet up with Billy Graham on Saturday morning at the Marriott Hotel in Boston. It was a mighty relief to finally meet and embrace the delegates in the hotel lobby on the Saturday morning. They had been through quite an ordeal. After days of being interrogated in Amman, upon their arrival in the US they had undergone further questioning, were photographed and had their fingerprints taken.

The delegation was extremely colourful with the Patriarch in his scarlet robes, the Ayatollah in his blue robes and large white turban and the Sunni sheik in his flowing black *abaya*, braided with gold. Dr Graham had become increasingly anxious as the week went on about the late arrival of the delegates. On the day, however, he welcomed them with great grace and kindness. The delegates clearly appreciated the opportunity to meet with one of the greatest Christian leaders in the world. After introductions they presented Dr Graham with gifts then told their own stories and the story of their people. Dr Graham listened intently and really seemed to understand the nature of the problem, its urgency and the need for rapid intervention.

After the delegates departed, I had a brief opportunity to discuss the meeting with Dr Graham and John Ackers before having to leave for the airport to return to the UK. In the meantime our Iraqi friends were in the good hands of Franklin's friends. Their programme now was much depleted, as they had missed most of the important meetings.

However, there were still two key appointments: meetings with former President Jimmy Carter and with the late Cardinal O'Connor. Both were arranged for Monday, so there was a free weekend ahead for the delegation. Not wanting the team to be disappointed and having the use of a private plane, the delegates were asked what they would like to do. They unanimously decided that they wanted to fly over the Niagara Falls. The following day their wish became true.

Meanwhile, back in the UK plans were developing well for their programme. Not wanting a repeat of the airport saga in New York we decided to enlist the help of the airport chaplains. They could not have been more helpful. As the delegates arrived in the UK they were met off the plane by the chaplains and given a rapid VIP entry. At arrivals they were met by scores of Iraqis living in Britain who had all turned out to welcome the eminent visitors. The first port of call was to be Coventry, a two-hour drive from the airport. I jokingly apologised for not having a private plane for them and assured them that next time I would try and do better!

The journey to Coventry was very important and we talked through their pain and fears. We assessed their shortened visit to the USA and talked through what was to happen in the days ahead. Their British programme was extremely full and would certainly be more taxing than what they had experienced in the US.

It was my first opportunity to begin to get to know Abdul Latif Humayeem. He is a very bright man with a wonderful laugh. After a while I said to him that I gathered he was the Billy Graham of Iraq. He appreciated the compliment, asking me how I knew this fact. I was perfectly up-front and said that the CIA had told us. He laughed again and replied that they would know because they listen to him every week.

As the delegates got out of the van at the Coventry hotel, a young youth shouted out, "Look, the Ayatollah has come to get us!" Little did this young man know that this indeed was one of the world's greatest Ayatollahs, nor that his family lived in fear and at great risk.

The following morning I took the religious leaders around Coventry Cathedral. They were all deeply impressed, especially by the story of the bombing of Coventry and its cathedral on the night of 14 November 1940. I explained to them how the Provost of the day, Dick Howard, had stood in the middle of the still-smouldering ruins of the Cathedral the next morning speaking words of peace. I told them of the significance of the two words the Provost wrote on the wall of the sanctuary, "Father, forgive," explaining that he had not written "Father forgive them" because we all need to be forgiven.

They looked at the charred cross made from the beams fallen from the burning roof and I told them the story of the Cross of Nails. Formed from nails that also fell from the roof, these nails had become a worldwide symbol of peace and reconciliation and the emblem of our international community committed to reconciliation. Abdul Latif responded in Arabic, "So this is why you care so much about the people of Iraq." This is why, because we as a community had suffered and knew without doubt that forgiveness is the only way forward. It is the only thing that will prevent the pain of the past from determining the future. I explained that this is what the cross was all about, us being reconciled to God through Jesus and being prepared to be Christ's ambassadors of reconciliation.

The Bishop of Coventry, who had been to Iraq and cared passionately about Iraq, hosted a wonderful lunch and meeting with local religious leaders. For the entire visit we were supported by two Coventry Iraqis. The first was Wafir Al Ghabban, an environmental engineer who with his English wife Karen and small son Sajad had become our closest friends.

I had met Wafir and Karen one night on a late train from London soon after I had arrived in Coventry, when I was still struggling to form links with Iraq. We got talking and soon realised how much we had in common. This was another one of those divine appointments, because Karen and Wafir have both continued to help us in our work. Wafir has spent many hours translating for the team and without him we would not have coped.

The other Coventry Iraqi was John Alpha, another wonderful man whose wife, a member of a Bedworth church, had heard some of my talks. She made contact with me telling how her husband John, a convert to Christianity, had become very disillusioned with the church during the Gulf

War as it had seemed to support military action against Iraq. He was now willing to work with us and do whatever he could to help.

After a well-attended public meeting the delegates came to a special service of evensong in the new cathedral where prayer was especially focused on Iraq. During that service we presented the delegates with a large Cross of Nails set in a piece of stone from the ruins of the old cathedral. The inscription on the brass plaque simply reads *"To the people of Iraq – Father, forgive."* Our guests, both Muslim and Christian, were later to say that this was the most moving moment of their entire visit. For the first time they realised that they were not a forgotten people and that there were people in Britain and even America who truly cared for them.

On Sunday, the Patriarch was taken to London to spend the day with his own Chaldean community in London. While in Coventry we organised a series of meetings with the local Islamic community. It was at this point that we discovered that the Ayatollah was extremely hesitant to meet with any Muslims, and always appeared to feel unwell immediately beforehand. This was clearly not just a co-incidence; it was fear-induced. I wondered why. Was it because he was Shia and they Sunni, or to do with difficult questions he might be asked about his own situation? Whatever it was, we wanted to be very sensitive and ensure that the Ayatollah was not forced to do anything that he felt uncomfortable about.

On a visit to Birmingham it was more difficult for the Ayatollah to retreat. He did therefore come to a meeting at the Saddam Hussein Mosque – not the most popular name in the centre of Birmingham. The mosque had been built with funds donated from the Iraqi leader in the 1980s. During the Gulf War it had come under constant attack until protection was provided by the parish church just across the road.

The Birmingham Islamic community were quite clearly delighted to be able to receive such a distinguished Iraqi delegation at their beloved mosque. After several more meetings in the Midlands we travelled to London for further religious and political meetings. The first was with the Archbishop of Canterbury, Dr George Carey, at Lambeth Palace, which got the programme off to a very good start. We were joined by Peter Price, the then Bishop of Kingston who had been part of the Episcopal delegation to Iraq.

The Archbishop was immediately able to identify with the delegates by talking about the two years he spent in Iraq as a wireless operator in the RAF during his national service. Dr Carey was totally supportive of all our efforts both in word and practice, and it was a great encouragement to the delegation to spend time with him. As a sign of their appreciation to the Archbishop, they presented him with the splendid robes of an Arab sheik.

Another meeting of importance was with the Marquess of Reading at the House of Lords. Lord Reading, otherwise known as Simon, was at that time heading an American-based flying hospital. It was literally a hospital on an airplane, with facilities to perform even the most complicated surgery. We had been trying to discern how best we could support the crumbling Iraqi health system.

One of the great needs was for clinicians to receive training in up-to-date surgical techniques, and the flying hospital was willing to explore ways which could facilitate this process. With Lord Reading was Chip Mann, the CEO of the project from the US. The delegates were fascinated to hear about this venture and invited Lord Reading and Chip Mann to come to Iraq to discuss how this idea could be taken further.

Our final meeting was to be at Chatham House, the Royal Institute of International Affairs. For many years Chatham House has been at the forefront of UK research and debate in international relations. The meeting had been widely publicised and there was a large audience, many of whom I recognised. Some there I trusted, and others were rather dubious characters.

The Patriarch mainly spoke, followed by Abdul Latif Humayeem. At the end of the speeches it was time, for questions. The first to be asked was by a member of the Al-Khoi foundation. Led by Joseph Al Khoi, this functioned as a Shia cultural organisation in London, but with a distinct Iraqi dissident agenda. Earlier in the week we were to have a meeting with the foundation but it was clear that none of the delegates wanted to attend. The meeting at Chatham House was soon to reveal why.

The person who asked the question spoke first in Arabic and then in English while two other members of the foundation unrolled a large banner. On it were the faces of over two hundred men, women and children, all of them clearly Shia. The Ayatollah was asked who these people were. He replied in classical Arabic, reciting text of the Koran. Again he was asked who these people were, again he replied with words of the Koran.

Eventually the person asking the question answered it: "They are all members of the Ayatollah's family who have either been killed or have disappeared." Again the Ayatollah replied with words from the Koran; his struggle was obvious. I intervened and asked those asking the questions to allow others the opportunity to speak, but by now the scene had been set. All present had seen a little of the anguish faced by the Iraqi people and particularly the plight of the suffering Shia majority. Not only were they being attacked from outside, they were also being attacked from within. The

Al-Khoi foundation wanted to show that the Ayatollah was part a persecuted group and that his visit to the UK was a façade, orchestrated by the Iraqi regime.

Later it was revealed that the Ayatollah also had a sister in London with whom he was afraid to make contact, although he had not seen her for over twenty years. One evening he asked if I could take him to see a doctor, which of course I was happy to do. He had been in severe pain for many months but treatment was not available. In his short visit to a London doctor there was not much that could be done but at least he now had some idea what was wrong and what limited action he could take to manage his condition.

During our moments together we were able to talk freely and openly about many issues including the struggles of his people. Whilst getting on very well with all the Iraqi religious leaders I felt particularly close to Ayatollah Al Sider. It was clear that he and his community had suffered much. He bore no bitterness and seemed to function purely at a spiritual level. Later I was to learn that the Ayatollah's entire family were under house arrest whilst he was out of the country.

The departure was quite emotional. Our friends could not thank us enough for the hospitality and kindness they had received. Yet I felt that we had received far more from them than we had given. They had exposed themselves, taken risks and allowed the people of Britain and America to see a little of the pain of their people. Although it would not be long before we would meet again, I knew they would soon be returning to a broken and hurting country, almost cut off from the rest of the world. It was seen as a rogue and enemy nation, but its people were our friends.

"Saddam of Prayer" mosaic outside the Al Kadhimia Mosque in central Baghdad.

The point of missile penetration at the Amiria Air Raid shelter.

The Saddam Mosque. The world's largest mosque under construction.

The Victory Parade ground, Baghdad. The arms of Saddam hold swords made from shot-down Iranian fighter planes. They sit on bases made from the helmets of dead Iranian soldiers.

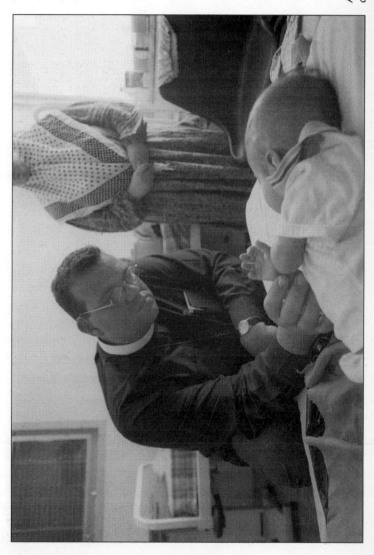

Another Iraqi child dying of cancer.

Pictures of children killed in a bomb blast on the walls of the Amiria Air Raid shelter.

Having fun with Iraqi children down by the River of Babylon.

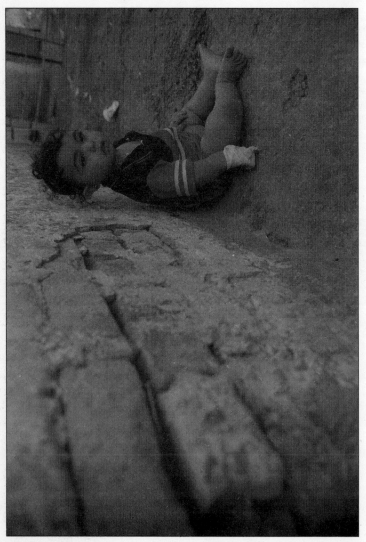

An Iraqi child sits by the open sewers in Old Baghdad.

Andrew White with his young friends in Old Baghdad.

A day out in Babylon. Andrew White and Tom Kay-Shuttleworth.

The 1999 delegation of British church leaders to Iraq. Left to right: Dr Charles Reed, Bishop Peter Price, Andrew White, Bishop Colin Bennetts, Tariq Aziz, Bishop Clive Handford, Riad Al Tahir, Archdeacon Ian Young.

The Iraqi religious leaders with Dr Billy Graham in Boston (September 1999). Front row left to right: Dr John Ackers, Sheik Abdul Latif Humayeem, Patriarch Raphael Bidawid I, Dr Billy Graham, Ayatollah Al Sider, Father Philip, Canon Andrew White.

Friday mid-day prayers in the ruins of Coventry Cathedral led by Archbishop Mar Thoma of Ninevah with Georges Sada. Left: Bishop of Coventry; right: Andrew White.

Meeting with Tariq Aziz. Left to right: Wafir Al-Ghabban, Georges Sada, Andrew White, Tariq Aziz, Tom Gillum, Tom Kay-Shuttleworth.

The presentation of the Coventry Cross of Nails to the people of Iraq. Left to right: Wafir Al Ghabban with Ayatollah Al Sider and Sheik Abdul Latif Humayeem, The Provost of Coventry The Very Reverend John Petty, The Rt Reverend Colin Bennetts Bishop of Coventry, Patriarch Raphael Bidawid I, Canon Andrew White and Father Philip representative of the Chaldean Church in Rome.

*The Iraqi religious leaders in the ruins of Coventry Cathedral
with the Cross of Nails.
Left to right: Ayatollah Al Sider, The Patriarch Bidawid I,
Canon Andrew White, Sheik Abdul Latif Humayeem.*

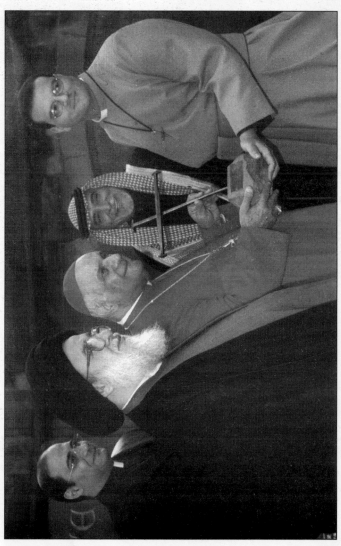

The Iraqi religious leaders in the ruins of Coventry Cathedral with the Cross of Nails. Left to right: Father Philip, Ayatollah Al Sider, The Patriarch Bidawid I, Sheik Abdul Latif Humayeem, Canon Andrew White.

Canon Andrew White in conversation with Iraqi foreign minister Naji Sabri (October 2002).

Chapter 5

Seeking to Help the People of Iraq

It had become perfectly clear that our involvement with Iraq was going to be long term. There was no instant solution to the political and humanitarian crisis that it was facing. We knew that one day things would have to change, but for that to happen there needed to be movement on both sides.

My policy has always been to try and live out the reality of the reconciling message of the cross. This, as I understand it, is the Coventry way. We will never make real progress if our work is simply advocacy. We need to fight hard for justice for the Iraqi people while being realistic about the nature of the regime.

We also need to maintain a positive and respectful relationship with our own government and Foreign Office. As the years went by there were fewer and fewer people who had any experience of Iraq. People like Sir Harold Walker, our last ambassador to Iraq, had long retired.

Although I may have disagreed with the British government, we always respected each other. On one occasion, I and the bishops who had been in Iraq with me were asked to give evidence to the Parliamentary International Development Committee. The Members of Parliament who heard our evidence were clearly distressed by the nature of the material that we presented. Not too long after we gave evidence, the same committee stated that they doubted whether it would ever be justified again to impose such sanctions on another nation.

We continued to keep in close contact with Hans von Sponeck who was finding his position increasingly untenable. Eventually he felt that he had no other option than to resign. In doing so he stated that the UN sanctions regime was both morally and ethically untenable. His resignation, though not unexpected, came as a huge shock to many people. He was the second UN humanitarian co-ordinator to resign in succession.

In the days following his resignation, von Sponeck was to inform us that the service we had together in the ruined Anglican church had been very significant in the final decision he had taken.

Meanwhile, plans were being made for another one of our delegates to Iraq, Charles Reed, to return. He had arranged to spend some time in Baghdad attached to the UN where he was to work at gathering statistics on the precise effects of the sanctions. Charles did eventually go back to Iraq for a six-week period. Sadly, by the time he arrived in Baghdad, Hans von Sponeck had already departed. Despite this setback, Charles managed to produce a significant publication entitled *A Decade of Sanctions* which looked in depth at the effect of sanctions in Iraq ten years after they were imposed.

On 14 November 2000, 60 years to the day that our cathedral was destroyed, we presented Count Hans von Sponeck with the Coventry International Prize for Peace and Reconciliation. In the ruins of a cathedral once bombed by the Germans, a German diplomat was awarded with this great honour. It was an outstanding day. Count von Sponeck with all his family around him finally felt vindicated for the actions he had taken in taking a stand against the UN and its sanctions programme.

The ceremony took place in two parts, firstly in the ruins of the old cathedral and then in the new cathedral prior to an amazing performance of Britten's *War Requiem*, written for the consecration of our new cathedral. On that day we learnt a very important fact about the von Sponeck family history. The father of Hans had been one of Hitler's senior generals but had refused to allow his troops to fight in Stalingrad. On his return to Germany he was imprisoned and later became part of the group who plotted to overthrow Hitler in 1944. A few days after the plot failed, Han's father was shot dead. Hans was then just a very young child, but had learned a great lesson from his father, which these many years later was to cost him his job.

A vital part of reconciliation is providing real help to those most in need. We had begun to discuss ways that we might be able to help those most vulnerable in Iraq. On a return trip to Baghdad I discussed the matter in depth with Dr Umeed Mubarak, the Minister of Health. We talked about the prospect of bringing the flying hospital into Baghdad and the specialities that local doctors needed training in. Now that the venture was a very real possibility, we began making arrangements for the team to visit Iraq. After many hours of discussion in the UK and America we were finally prepared to take a team out on a reconnaissance trip.

The delegation was to include the Marquess of Reading, Chip Mann the CEO from the US and the medical and technical directors, Loren and Dwight Lorenz who just happened to be married to each other. What the Iraqis were not aware of was the fact that Chip Mann had been one of President George Bush's Sr private staff. What's more, President Bush himself had been involved in the launching of the Flying Hospital which was owned by Pat Robertson of the Christian Broadcasting Network.

Our journey from Amman to Baghdad was interesting. On such a journey you have a lot of time to get to know each other well. As we drove along the desert motorway we heard stories of Chip's exploits with President Bush including from the time of the Gulf War. Now we were taking this senior Bush aid to the country that his boss had played a major role in trying to destroy. The biggest problem was to come. As we arrived at the entrance of the Al Rasheed Hotel, Chip was determined not to walk over the face of his former employer, George Bush. It was one of the few moments of light relief watching Chip hop, skip and jump over the wonderful mosaic of the 41st President of the USA.

By this stage in the history of my travel to Iraq, Georges Sada, our brother in Baghdad would have everything ready by the time we arrived. Our cars would be there, at least part of the programme arranged and there would be one man, in Georges, who actually knew what he was doing. Georges in addition to being the President of the Protestant Churches of Iraq was also a former Air vice Marshall. As one of Iraq's most senior Air Force Officers, Georges was very well connected. In the Gulf War he had been the officer with particular responsibility for the care of the prisoners of war. He was a passionate Christian. At every opportunity he would share the gospel. He also headed up the Bible Society and coordinated much of the youth ministry. On one occasion he led the Iraqi delegation to an international conference of our Community of the Cross of Nails at Coventry Cathedral. Also travelling with him was the Archbishop of Nineveh. At this symposium there was some concern amongst both the Israeli and Iraqi delegations that they would be in the same seminar group as each other, both being from the Middle East.

In the end they got on brilliantly. During this conference Georges was officially presented with a personal Cross of Nails and appointed as the head of our community in Iraq. Another paradox in the life of Georges, as we recognised this great man as a true reconciler.

We visited all the usual sites and people that we had to visit but concentrated on liaison with the hospitals. The medical staff were desperate for knowledge, equipment and drugs. Many of them had been trained in the UK or the US; they were highly skilled and well educated but very out of date. The sanctions system did not just affect equipment and medicines but also supplies of books, periodicals and medical journals. Everything in the library predated the Gulf War.

As the medical team spent time at the hospital, I went off with Lord Reading to meet up again with some of the religious leaders who had come to the UK. First we went to the Chaldean Cathedral to ensure that the Cross of Nails from Coventry had arrived safely. I was rather concerned that it was not there.

Later at lunch with the Patriarch I asked him where the Cross was. He smiled and showed me to his car; there it was on his back seat. The Patriarch went on to explain that the plaque said "to the people of Iraq." He therefore used to take it around the country with him, placing it on the altar and telling people that they were not forgotten. This was a very moving story, and enough to make us feel that there was indeed a purpose in our actions.

Returning to Amman, I talked through our work in Iraq with Lord Reading. He is one of my closest confidants and a patron of our International Centre for Reconciliation.

It was quite clear that the work was increasing rapidly. If we were to keep on top of all the developments I needed a member of staff to assist me. A person of exceptional calibre would be needed to perform such a support role, but it was not really the kind of post that you could advertise. I did not suppose there were a huge number of people who would be eager for a job in Iraq.

We talked through the kind of profile of the person we were looking for. We needed a man; you could not have a woman dealing with such senior Islamic leaders. The person would need to be young, preferably unattached with a good knowledge of politics and diplomacy.

Lord Reading was convinced that he knew the right person, a young man called Thomas Kay-Shuttleworth. Educated at Eton and Cambridge, he had spent time working as a researcher for a Member of Parliament, he was also working for a charity caring for street children in Russia and the Ukraine.

On returning to England I immediately made contact with Tom and we arranged to meet at my club in London. At my first meeting with Tom I knew he was just the kind of person we needed. He is first and foremost a person of great faith, very bright and committed to working for reconciliation.

Once Tom was on board he proved to be not just a great work colleague but also a wise friend. He immediately started accompanying me on trips to Iraq and quickly formed good working relationship with all who we had to engage with. By now we often had other people also travelling with us, people who were concerned about Iraq and wanted also to make known the story of this ancient people.

Fellow-travellers were always much appreciated, especially on the 14-hour road journey. The most memorable and moving of all these visits was when our friends Karen, Wafir and four-year-old Sajad accompanied us. Wafir had not been to Iraq for over twenty years and he was not even sure if it was safe for him to return, while Karen and Sajad had never visited. Crossing the border that day between Jordan and Iraq was a very different experience, a time of real joy. Sajad immediately was taken by all of the huge pictures of "Noah," as he saw them. From this day we had a new pseudonym for the evil dictator. Also travelling with us on that visit was Tom Gillum, the vicar of St Stephen's, Westbourne Grove in London.

On this trip we combined the usual visits with some more interesting activities. We went to Babylon and there viewed the ancient ruins that Saddam was rebuilding. Each brick was inscribed with his name, following the example of Nebuchadnezzar. Overlooking this ancient site was a splendid building, which our minder forbade us to take pictures of, as it was an "official guest house." Georges in his usual way summed up the situation: "That's the name for Saddam's palace." It was amazing how in public open spaces you were often prevented from taking pictures in a certain direction.

Another interesting visit was soon to follow this one. In December of the year 2000 I was to visit Iraq twice in one week. Having made the journey back from Iraq on the Thursday, I was to travel back on Monday. I had a pre-arranged visit to discuss some very serious issues and then was asked to be part of the first flight into Iraq since the Gulf War. Accompanying me would be a British television crew.

A French Catholic priest, Father Benjamin, was organising this trip with parliamentarians from across Europe, and was insistent that he wanted me to accompany them. We left Birmingham airport on Monday morning and flew to Paris with a very tight transfer time of just over an hour in which to cross Paris to the other airport.

Disaster was soon to strike, because the television camera appeared not to have arrived from Birmingham. With forty-five minutes before departure from the other airport, we had to try to find this camera or another one. As usual it was our office in Coventry that had to deal with this little problem. After contacting various French television stations they finally tracked down an available camera, paid for its hire and had it delivered by courier.

We arrived at Charles de Gaulle airport with fifteen minutes to spare, giving instructions to all of the airport staff to allow the camera to come straight through to the departure gate. It was now time for departure, and everybody apart from us had boarded. We were just being told that there was no more time to wait when a man came sprinting towards the gate with a large television camera. It was that day that I discovered that our staff at Coventry really could perform miracles!

Meanwhile, we were still desperate to try and do something positive to really help the Iraqi people. We had already raised funds to help some of those whom we knew were most desperate, but this was not enough. The saga regarding the flying hospital seemed never ending. Getting definite answers about dates for the mission proved near impossible and just as we were about to finalise arrangements for the venture, the owners of the flying hospital decided the whole operation was far too expensive and they would need to find a buyer or major funder. Determined not to let the people of Iraq down, Tom and I returned to Baghdad to find out from the Minister of Health how we could best help him.

We were relieved to discover that what he really wanted was not the flying hospital but training for his haematology team in the techniques of bone marrow transplantation. Dr Umeed Mubarak explained to us that for several years they had been requesting help from various governments but none of them had been able to deliver. We already knew how serious the level of leukaemia was, particularly amongst young people.

One of the things that we learnt early on in our dealings with Iraq was that nothing happened quickly. However urgent a matter was, and however quickly the Iraqi Government said they needed our help, we knew it would always take months before the ball rolled in Baghdad. The reason for this bureaucracy was not easy to discern, but probably had a lot to do with the need for Saddam's personal approval. Accompanied with very bad communications, this meant that there is no such thing as a prompt reply from Iraq. At times we would wait for days for a reply to come through to Dr Amin, the head of the Iraqi interest section in London. He himself would be as frustrated as we were but was also powerless.

After intensive discussions with the medical team at the Al Mansour Hospital we were satisfied that we had sufficient information to begin the planning of the training programme. We not only needed to find the right hospital to provide the training, we also needed to find the total funding of the project. This would include cost of travel, accommodation and further training materials. After much research we finally met with Dr Tony Darbyshire from the Princess Diana Children's Hospital in Birmingham, a paediatric haematologist with much experience in performing bone marrow transplants. He agreed that the Children's Hospital would be prepared to carry out the training programme for the Iraqi team.

The process of finding the funding was given an early major boost by a donation from Sir Richard Branson. Richard Branson has been a long-term supporter of the International Centre for Reconciliation and had a particular interest in helping children.

As in all of our negotiations with Iraq, the process leading to the commencement of the project was long and complex. Further visits were made to Baghdad to try and clarify the

situation. We were very fortunate to have the help of
Michelle Berry, a young woman from South Africa who
volunteered to come and work with us while she was
completing her MA in Peace and Reconciliation at the
University of Coventry. The hours that Michelle put into
this project were phenomenal. Further funding was secured
from a charity called Aid for Iraqi Children and from the
Catholic relief agency CAFOD.

After many months of tireless negotiations, we eventually
were able to invite one of the Iraqi doctors to England to
take the plans further. Dr Abdul Majeed eventually arrived
in June 2001, another kind and gentle person who could not
thank us enough for the opportunity that had been given to
him. Once again my friends Karen and Wafir Al Ghabban
provided the most amazing hospitality for him, making him
feel most welcome, while Dr Darbyshire went out of his way
to ensure that Dr Majeed had as constructive a visit as
possible. The stories that Dr Majeed told about the deterior-
ating conditions of his hospital were most disturbing, as
were the accounts of their difficulties in getting even some
of the most essential medicine and equipment.

From the time of Dr Majeed's successful visit, there were
further months of waiting and bureaucracy. In the meantime Tom and I made several return visits to Iraq and on one
occasion Tom visited alone. Our Embassy in Jordan continued to be very helpful in making arrangements for visas to
be issued and Georges' son-in-law Nabil looked after all the
arrangements in Amman. Permission was finally gained for
a team of six to come to the UK for training in bone marrow
transplantation techniques.

It was to be over a year until the team arrived on
5 September 2002. Prior to that, an event was to take place
that would change the course of history and complicate
even further our involvement with Baghdad.

Chapter 6

Nine-eleven:
the Day that Changed History

On the 11 September 2001 I was sitting in my study in the undercroft of Coventry Cathedral, making final arrangements for my journey to Baghdad the following day. I was to travel with a BBC reporter who was going to do a feature on our work in Iraq for the Sunday Programme on BBC Radio 4. The reporter was already in Amman and I had arranged for our car to bring him to the airport the following night, from where we would travel directly from the airport to Iraq.

At 2.30 pm I was listening to the radio, when suddenly the programme was interrupted with a news flash: an aeroplane had flown into the side of the World Trade Centre. Moments later the second attack was announced. Immediately all of my phones (and I have many) started to ring. The calls were from journalists wanting to know my views on what was happening and whether I thought that these attacks were linked to what was happening in the Middle East.

Apart from our work in Iraq I had also been very involved with the Israeli-Palestinian conflict. I had been in Israel just days before when Abu Ali Mustapha, the leader of the Popular Front for the Liberation of Palestine had been assassinated. I was also aware of the increasing influence of various Islamic extremist groups, not least the Al Qaida movement headed by the renegade Saudi, Osama Bin Ladin. It was obviously a very serious situation, and no mere accident. It was also clear that I was unlikely to fly to Amman the following day.

That evening the enormity of the crisis started to became obvious. By now the Pentagon had also been attacked and another plane had come down in Pennsylvania. I began to think about the implication that this attack would have on Iraq. To me it was obvious that these terrible attacks were not the work of Iraq, yet there was a very high risk that Iraq would be the target of reprisals.

The following morning as the whole world awoke to the reality of this terrible catastrophe I phoned Allan Gaulty, then the Director of the North Africa and Middle East Department of the Foreign and Commonwealth Office. He made it quite clear to me that as things were at the moment I should not go to Iraq. I had to take his advice. What's more, all flights to the Middle East had been cancelled.

My focus for today had to be looking after the pastoral needs of those affected by this tragedy. Our new dean at the Cathedral had only been in office for one week and suddenly he was also faced with having to make a response to this calamity. I briefed our senior staff meeting, before walking into the ruins of our old cathedral. Already people were beginning to bring flowers.

As I stood in the midst of this evocative place of worship and reconciliation, my mind immediately went to the morning after the bombing of Coventry. It was on 15 November 1940 that the then Provost Dick Howard spoke about forgiving those who had done this and becoming their friend. As I watched people come and lay their flowers, I wondered how many of them really realised what this place was about. I asked myself the same question. Could I really say those words "Father, forgive" and call for forgiveness today?

The 11th of September was a Tuesday; the following Friday we had arranged to have a special act of prayer and remembrance. As I walked up into the main body of the cathedral that day, I was completely taken aback by the mass of people. Thousands were gathered, including our Lord Mayor, the leader of our city council and other dignitaries. There were many Americans also in the congregation, many who had travelled considerable distances to be with us. This was not unique to Coventry, because in cathedrals and churches across the UK and the world the same acts of remembrance and prayer were going on.

As we prayed for victims and their families, we also prayed for our enemies, asking God to give us the grace to forgive. I was also thinking continually of Iraq and wondering whether the people of that broken nation would at some time have to pay the price for this act of terror.

On the following Monday, the 17th of September, I finally flew to Amman in preparation for my travel to Iraq. A twice-weekly flight from Amman to Baghdad had been established but in the light of the 11th of September this had also been postponed. I therefore organised that our usual driver should come and drive me directly to Baghdad. Over the years of doing this journey, I had managed to perfect the routine of travel to make it as bearable as possible. I would arrive in Amman at 1 am and sleep in the car until 4.30 am, at which point we were at the border. An hour later we would recommence our journey. I would try and get some more sleep and at 3.30 pm we would arrive in Baghdad.

When we arrived in Baghdad on Tuesday 18 September, the atmosphere of the city seemed strangely different. Georges was as usual waiting for me at the Al Rasheed Hotel.

He had already organised much of the programme and I was to see Tariq Aziz that evening. I had the normal government cars and people to look after me but they seemed strangely quiet on this visit. Georges explained that people were very afraid, sure that in some way they would face recriminations for what happened in New York and Washington exactly a week ago. Evidently many of the senior government officials and members of the Revolutionary Council had fled Baghdad after the news of the terror attacks. They were afraid that reprisals would be quick and that Iraq would be the target.

My minder from the Ministry of Protocol this time was Hameed, who told me that I was the first official visitor to Iraq since the events of 9/11. It was therefore going to be a very important week. I would have to talk a lot to the Iraqi media because they would want to know what the world was thinking about Iraq at this time. Saddam Hussein had not helped matters by being the only head of state not to condemn the terrible acts of the previous week. He had implied that America had got what it deserved and what was destined to come in recompense for all of its own evil acts of violence. This was exactly the kind of message that the West did not need to hear from Saddam at this difficult time.

Tariq Aziz had moved out of his dilapidated office some time ago and now was based in a large palace very close to the Al Rasheed. The external architecture of this palace was splendid, with all the grace and beauty of the best of oriental architecture. Within the octagonal lobby, there was a thick red carpet on the main staircase and the largest chandelier that I have ever seen. The walls of the entrance hall were gilded with gold and the building felt cool in the midst of the blistering heat of Iraqi summer. But as one left the lobby the whole nature of the decor changed very considerably. Most of the building was very shabby, with poorly fitted carpet, exposed wires and polystyrene-tiled ceilings. So inside the shell of a palace was another reality.

Iraq was a nation in fear and I had no idea what Tariq Aziz's response would be to me. As I entered his room, he stood to greet me and said loudly, "Andrew, tell them we had nothing to do with it. We are revolutionaries, not terrorists!" Without thinking much about my response I said to him, "Your Excellency, it doesn't matter whether you are terrorists or revolutionaries, they are still coming to get you."

For an hour Mr Aziz explained to me how it was really the Americans who were the terrorists. He gave me a lesson in reconstructionist history, starting with Vietnam and working through to Chile. He spoke of how the Americans had put terrorists into power and how they always regretted it. Even though I did not agree with what he was saying, his encyclopaedic knowledge of international affairs was impressive. Aziz continued to tell me what Iraq meant by being a revolutionary state, saying that he did not condone the attacks of 9/11 but then made reservations about this statement.

By this stage the main blame was already being directed at Al Qaida and in particularly at its leader Osama Bin Ladin. Yet President George Bush was already beginning to talk of the "Axis of Evil" and the need to go to the ends of the earth to rid the world of terrorism. I asked Aziz if he thought Iraq would be attacked. His answer was clear: "We are already attacked every day by America, both by their planes in our no-fly zone and by sanctions." He continued by saying that if they were attacked they would fight, and fight hard.

For the past three years our work in Iraq had been very complex. We had established good relationships, made known the plight of the Iraqi people and tried to help practically. Nevertheless the situation remained desperate, and even while the situation in Baghdad was beginning to slightly stabilise, in the rest of Iraq things continued to deteriorate.

There was also a rapidly developing social elite, those who had done well out of sanctions by the development of a black market. In Baghdad you could find almost anything you wanted, if you had the money to pay for it. The Iraqi dinar was holding its value at about 2,000 dinars to the US dollar, many of the cars now had windscreens and there was food in the markets. The majority of people, however, continued to live in total poverty, struggling to find even the most basic living requirements.

My meeting with Tariq Aziz was as usual very friendly but deeply worrying. There was still no concept of Iraq needing to do anything to change the attitude of the world toward it, or of being willing to engage with the international community on the key issue of weapons of mass destruction. At the same time there was no evidence of the UN, Britain and America being willing to seriously engage with Iraq about the continuing humanitarian crisis.

Later that week I continued in my normal discussions with other political and religious leaders. My meetings with the Ayatollah were always encouraging and took place at a profoundly spiritual level. He condemned the atrocities of the previous week, making clear that such actions and behaviour are always against the will of the Almighty.

The Ayatollah lived in a large building in the centre of Baghdad, very close to the spectacular shrine of Al Kadhimia. His students and followers obviously held him in the highest regard. Each time we visited we would go through the same ritual. First we would be shown into his reception room; we would wait a few minutes as his students would line up outside. At the arrival of the Ayatollah, the students would pay homage to him in a formal line. He would then choose which of them should be with us at the meeting and also wait on us. We would then be brought a cold drink which would be followed by Arab coffee and then a huge plate of fruit with a knife.

The meeting would always begin with the offering of praise to Allah for being able to meet together. He would continue by talking of the importance of the heavenly religions in working together. He never failed to mention how significant his visit to England was for him and his people. At no point would he ever discuss things which were overtly political, not even regarding the problems of sanctions. My visits were always spoken of being of utmost importance to him and his community. I was however always aware that my minders were also with us. This did not seem to be an issue of great concern to him but it did constrict our freedom of conversation.

Each time I visited the Ayatollah I would take him a little gift and always received a large one in return. Sometimes it would be several volumes of his latest scholarly work; on other occasions I would be presented with an *abaya* (a traditional sheik's robe), embroidered with fine gold thread. On another occasion the entire team was presented with fine pure wool cloth, beautifully wrapped. This level of immense generosity was most humbling for us, as was the extent of hospitality that we were shown wherever we visited.

As I returned to the Al Rasheed I was informed that the journalist Mona was looking for me. I was always pleased to see her, despite my low opinion of her newspaper. I had much to talk to her about because I had been writing to her father who was receiving medical treatment in the north of England. His letters were always extremely honest; if he were to have written such material from Iraq his life and the lives of his family would have been in grave danger. He spoke of the butchery, torture and killing that took place at the hands of Saddam and his Republican Guard. He told me stories of what had happened to his friends who had dared to ask questions and the way the whole of Iraq lived in fear and dread of the regime. Each letter he signed as "Tigris Son."

On a previous visit, Mona had presented me with one of her bright paintings, and knowing how her father signed his letters to me, she signed the picture, "Tigris Daughter." The Bishop of Coventry and I had established a playful ritual of giving the picture to each other for birthdays and Christmas. That was until my young son saw the picture and decided it was a picture of a Barbie doll, and he wanted it.

As we sat in a quiet corner of the hotel with the piano playing, this time badly. I asked her what she really thought of her president and country. This was not the kind of question I had ever asked anybody in Iraq before, but I knew we were in a relatively safe place and nobody was looking. She answered immediately "We all love our president; he is a strong, good man."

I made it clear that her father did not quite see him like that. There was a moment of silence. Tears begun to roll down her full cheeks and eventually she spoke. "None of us wanted this, we didn't want to go into Kuwait, we don't want to hate the rest of the world, we don't want to live in this hellish prison, and it is entirely his fault." The armour had cracked, that armour which enables Saddam to be elected with 100% of the vote, and which enables journalists like Mona to vote the president's evil son as the journalist of the millennium.

The armour is about self-preservation. In Iraq there is no room for opposition. Those who ask why the people of Iraq have not risen up against Saddam do not understand the nature of the regime. There is no room for opposition in this ancient land. The iron rod of the new Nebuchadnezzar is all-embracing and all-controlling.

We walked in the garden so we could talk privately. Against the sunset I could see the victory parade monument, modelled from shot-down Iranian fighter planes. The arms of Saddam held swords and huge nets full of Iranian solders' helmets, the same helmets that covered the ground around this monument like cobblestones. The dear people of Iraq had suffered so much, from their leader and the rest of the world. As I looked in the other direction there was the latest palace and immediately ahead on the former airport the Saddam Mosque, soon to be the biggest in the world, filled the evening skyline.

Mona was earning $4 a month, twice what many would earn. Half a mile in the other direction I knew that by now children would be gathering around the closing stalls of the market by the barracks to see if any of the solders had dropped scraps of food. The ordinary people of this great land were the suffering forgotten. More than ever before, the pain of this desolation was becoming almost unbearable. Why was I here, and what was I doing? It was over three years since I first arrived in Iraq and yet again the clouds of war were gathering. The people were still hurting and what we had done for them was minimal, only some food, medicine and money here and there.

Later in the week I returned to my favourite place, the Mother Theresa home. As I entered, it seemed very quiet and I knew something was different. I looked for Ahmed and Immanuel, but neither of them was there. "Sister, where are Ahmed and Immanuel?" I asked, fearing the worst. The response was very encouraging, however: a visiting Australian doctor had seen them and was convinced that they needed surgical help if they were to ever survive later in life. He had then arranged for them to be flown to Australia for at least a year's treatment. Whilst I was so sad not to see them both, I knew that this was a wonderful answer to prayer.

As I played with some of the children, a British-educated neighbour asked me why I kept coming back to Iraq. "You must be crazy," he said. One of the sisters sternly replied for me: "You must not say that. Father Andrew is here because God wants him to be here." There was my answer; I was here because God wanted me to be here. Even if the reasoning did not quite add up, this was where I was meant to me.

So much of the work of reconciliation is about incarnational ministry: being prepared to be the hands, feet and mouth of Jesus. I remembered the words of one of my friends preaching about intercession. He described it as bringing God into the godless. This was what we were trying to do. Bringing God into this dark abyss, to try and bring about change and set these captives free.

The year following 9/11 proved to be most difficult. Not only were there wars and rumours of war, there was the escalating crisis in the Middle East conflict. Negotiations between Israelis and Palestinians had all but broken down and I was increasingly spending my time shuttling between Yasser Arafat held in his compound in Ramalah and the Israeli Foreign Ministry in Jerusalem. Then there were the six weeks of negotiating in Bethlehem during the siege of the Church of the Nativity.

Throughout this time we were trying to persevere with our humanitarian projects in Iraq and keep on top of the developing political situation. It was very difficult communicating with Baghdad; communications between Iraq and Jerusalem are particularly difficult and always are potentially risky for the party in Iraq. Despite these risks Georges would still make contact with me and brief me on what was happening.

In the many hours that I would spend in the Mukarta (compound) in Ramalah I would often discuss Iraq with Yasser Arafat. He had been one of the few Arab leaders who had supported Saddam in the Gulf War. Backing the wrong side was to have quite serious consequences for him.

There were beginning to be stories of Saddam paying money to families of Palestinian suicide bombers, and I tried to persuade Yasser Arafat to clearly disassociate himself from such funding. I explained that the humanitarian crisis was even worse in Iraq than Palestine, yet Saddam was trying to capitalise on the developing *intifada*. Baghdad was full of pictures of Palestinian "martyrs" and Saddam had formed a new army called the Al Quads Brigade (Jerusalem Brigade). With 2 million members, the army seemed to be made up predominantly of women.

Meanwhile, back in Coventry the team at the International Centre for Reconciliation were working hard on the final arrangements for the bone marrow training to begin. Michelle Berry had planned things brilliantly and despite the growing tension between Iraq and the West, our embassy in Jordan continued to be very cooperative about the project. Visas were finally issued, Georges helped with practical arrangements and the team finally arrived in the UK on 5 September 2002. As usual the chaplaincy team at Heathrow Airport assured that our medical guests had a smooth VIP entry into the country. I was just on my way back to Israel and could only quickly greet the team as they arrived in Coventry. Dr Majeed and his colleagues were delighted to finally be in England. We embraced each other and I promised to meet up with them as soon as I returned.

At the last moment the Iraqi government had decided that one of the team was not going to be allowed to come, with no explanation for this last-minute decision. I knew not to ask any questions. The team settled in well, staying at the Woodbrooke, a Quaker College in Birmingham. They were shown such gracious hospitality there and immediately made to feel like one of the family. Dr Darbyshire and his team went out of their way to ensure that they received all the training needed in a limited space of time. While the team were with us I returned again to Iraq and was able to give a positive report to the team's colleagues and the Minister of Health, Dr Umeed Mubarak.

The final night of the team's stay in Birmingham, I took them all out for dinner. It was an emotional meeting and an even more emotional departure. The one lady in the team, a 52-year-old nurse, sobbed as she left us; she did not want to return. All she could keep saying was that we had such love and freedom here.

Love and freedom are qualities that we in the Western world take for granted. As we departed there was a sense that our friends were returning not just to a totalitarian state but one which was soon to be in the grips of another violent war.

Chapter 7

The Final Return

By September 2002 the US and her allies were now confident that the situation in Afghanistan was under control. With regime change now complete, attention was now turning to Iraq. The UN resolution 1441 was now in place and negotiations were underway regarding the return of the weapons inspectors.

I had received word from Baghdad that Tariq Aziz and the Foreign Minister Naji Sabri wanted to see me. The week in question I had a journalist and photographer following me around in Israel and Palestine. They were also very keen to come to Iraq and permission was gained for them to join me. Also joining the delegation were two former army chaplains, Michael Smith and John Holliman both now vicars within the diocese of Chichester. I was hoping that their assessment of the situation would be helpful in reaching a conclusion about the escalating crisis.

I have travelled several times from Jerusalem to Baghdad, a journey which is obviously uncommon. Entrance into Iraq is prohibited if there is an Israeli stamp in the passport. The journalists and I left Jerusalem after breakfast and drove to the Allenby Bridge, but soon discovered that you could no

longer obtain Jordanian visas there. We were due to meet
the deputy Ambassador at the Embassy in just two hours
before taking the Royal Jordanian flight to Baghdad, which
now flew twice weekly, and was heavenly compared to the
road journey. When I was unable to persuade the Jordanian
border police, I managed to ring the Jordanian Minister of
Interior whose mobile phone number I had been supplied
with by a Palestinian friend in London. In minutes we were
in the car of the Palestinian Ambassador being driven to our
embassy in Amman.

After our briefing session we made our way to the airport
for the flight. Georges had been waiting for us in Amman so
that he could fully brief us before entering Iraq. As usual he
went the extra mile. His son-in-law Nabil had organised our
tickets and all arrangements seemed to be in hand.

The flight to Baghdad was uneventful and to my delight
we were met by Jabber. He had heard that I was returning
and had managed to gain permission to be my minder. The
first thing I wanted to know was how his son was. This was
the poor man who had followed us around in the hospitals
trying to find medicine for his young son. The news was not
good; his son's condition had deteriorated significantly with
no medication available to control his epilepsy, and he had
died four months previously. There was not much I could
say. Yet another child victim in Iraq: a further statistic to add
to the hundreds of thousands of children who had died
unnecessarily since the Gulf War.

If the atmosphere had been strained after 9/11, now it was
intensely fearful. Immediately people were asking me when
the next war would begin, hoping I mysteriously had some
answer to their worst fear. The staff at the Al Rasheed were
resigned to their fate. "Only God can help us now," said
Mustapha, the reception manager.

We had breakfast in Jerusalem, lunch in Amman and now

dinner in Baghdad: three cities, three different countries and three nations all on the brink of disaster.

The people of Iraq had now resigned themselves to further devastation. Before, people had hoped for a better future, but it had not come. The whole issue of sanctions had always brought outrage, but now they were asking deeper questions and not merely condemning the West.

It was clear that over my four years of visiting Iraq, people were beginning to trust me. In Arab cultures you have to earn respect and trust. I had learned, too, that my initial assessment of the situation had not been totally accurate. There are many layers to Iraqi society and to the problems that it faces.

Despite this awareness I was not prepared for what I was to face in my visit of autumn 2002. The leadership was now fairly desperate. They knew that the threat of the US and her allies was real. In part they wanted to avoid confrontation but on the other hand were prepared to fight any aggressor head-on.

I was used to a large number of meetings with senior Iraqi politicians on any visit but this time there were more than usual. We began by visiting the minister of AwQaf (Ministry of Religious Affairs) whom I had met on many occasions before. He was not a particularly inspiring person, fairly quiet and without much influence. Like the other members of the Revolutionary Guard he wore military uniform.

The minister began the meeting not with a tirade against the West but with thanks for the response of the Church of England to the pending crisis between Iraq and the West. "Dr Rowan Williams is a very good man and Archbishop Carey, and we are very happy with the Bishop of Coventry and the Bishop of Bath and Wells. The Bishop of Oxford has also been very good." The list continued like a page of *Crockford's Clerical Directory*. I was somewhat taken back by the extent of the minister's knowledge of the positions of Anglican episcopacy.

These thanks were reiterated through the week. The following meeting was with the speaker of the Iraqi parliament, just a few days before the parliament voted overwhelmingly against allowing the weapons inspectors to return. Everybody knew that this decision would be overturned by the president but they had made their point. The constant refrain was that Iraq had nothing to hide and that the inspectors could come and look but they would find nothing. The other theme amongst many was that they would fight back, and fight back hard.

Another significant development since the Gulf War was that people had increasingly turned to religion. Iraq had traditionally been a very secular society but that is no longer the case. The mosques and churches are full. Many Muslim women now wear Islamic dress and people speak openly of how their faith in God is enabling them to continue.

As on all my visits to Iraq, I went to see Hanna at the Anglican Church. Here also there has been change. Despite there still being no minister at the church, people now flock to the building in their hundreds. On St George's Day over two thousand people visited the church. St George is much revered throughout the Middle East and not just by Christians.

Hanna regularly prays in the church and at service times you can hear hymns played loud over the speakers. It is a bizarre experience to be driving down a Baghdad street and hear carols from Coventry Cathedral blaring! I did suggest to Hanna that it might be more appropriate to play hymns in the vernacular. Georges supplied some Arabic Christian music which from time to time was also played.

The other thing that Georges had done as head of the Iraqi Bible Society was to provide Hanna free of charge with large supplies of Arabic Christian literature and Bibles. Hanna had now established a flourishing little Christian book shop and with the additional revenue he was employing a full-time gardener to help look after the grounds. I am not sure what the Bishop of Cyprus and Gulf would have made of such entrepreneurial skills!

As we were leaving the church I met a group of women going into the church. One of them spoke good English and we began to have a conversation. She explained that some of her friends were actually Muslims but every lunch time they would leave work and go together to pray at St George's.

The new commitment to faith and religious fervour was seen across the board, not least amongst the Shia community which amounts to 67% of Iraq's population. I paid my customary visit to the Ayatollah Al Sider and was welcomed in his usual gracious manner. This time I was presented with a fine mohair *abaya* braided with gold. As usual the conversation with the Ayatollah functioned very much at a spiritual level with no talk of politics. He continued to give thanks to God for our friendship and for his visit to the US and UK.

The meeting with the Sunni leader, sheik Abdul Latif Humayeem was as usual full of laughter. It never ceased to amaze me how happy this man managed to remain despite the tragedy all around. He had recently become the President of the Popular Islamic Conference and was based at their new offices in the centre of Baghdad. As far as I could tell this was another Iraqi creation, as the organisation's literature barely mentioned that there were other Arab countries in the world.

The sheik was also full of thanks for the support of the Church of England and wanted to know when the new Archbishop of Canterbury would be visiting. Dr Williams' words had been closely followed; he certainly had made many friends in Iraq.

The sheik was known to be one of Saddam's closest confidants and had even gone on Hajj (pilgrimage to Mecca) on his behalf. As we prepared to leave I was asked, "Do you want to see the President?" I had known that this question was inevitable but however much I thought about it, I was unprepared to answer. Saying "No" might be seen as an insult, but meeting him could seriously compromise our work with our own government, as Bishop Colin and I had made clear to Dr Amin, the head of the Iraqi Interest Section in London just before this visit to Iraq.

I managed to reply in a noncommittal way, by stating that the President must be far too busy to see somebody like me. As we departed I was informed that a special gift would be delivered to the Al Rasheed for Dr Rowan Williams, Archbishop Carey and me. Later that day three more *abayas* arrived at the Al Rasheed. Once again they were made of best-quality cashmere and gold braid.

The other key meetings were all political. The palace where Tariq Aziz was based remained unfinished, but he remained as secure in his position as he had for the past four decades. Aziz is culturally a Chaldean Christian and one of Saddam's old revolutionary colleagues. Very few people have survived as he has. Even members of the President's own family have succumbed to the sword but Aziz has remained as Iraq's face to the West. Tariq Aziz is no pushover – he has ardently rejected Western policy and on one occasion before the Gulf War in 1990 even refused to accept a hand-delivered letter from President George Bush Sr.

On one of my previous visits to Tariq Aziz he reminded me of his love of things British and mentioned his liking for HP sauce. I therefore presented him with three bottles of his favourite sauce. As I gave them to him, I pointed out the picture on the bottle of the Houses of Parliament and said that they were not very happy with him at that moment.

Before getting on to the serious issue of how Iraq was to respond to resolution 1441, Aziz complimented me on my work in Palestine. He said that he had been following it very closely and that the Zionist aggressors needed to be defeated. On this visit the links between the situation in Iraq and Palestine were referred to constantly.

When it came to the discussion on Iraq, Aziz stated that the weapons inspectors were welcome but that the country would not entertain the espionage and looting of antiquities which took place on previous inspections. At this point, he asked me to head up a team to monitor the work of the weapons inspectors, ensuring me that I would be given an office, transport, accommodation and everything else that I needed. He suggested that we could get other religious leaders involved, who could come for two or three weeks at a time. While there may have been some value in the idea, it seemed that establishing such a process would only compli- cate further the delicate political and diplomatic exercise of weapons inspection.

As we came to the end of our meeting, Aziz made clear that they were ready for war and were not going to go easily. He acknowledged the limit of Iraq's military strength com- pared to the might of Britain and America but declared that this would not deter them in the battle. At the end of the meeting, those with us left the room and I remained with the Deputy Prime Minister for a time of private conversation.

I left this meeting feeling positively depressed. It was quite obvious that this escalating crisis was steering out of control. The future was now very bleak. The avoidance of war even after the entry of the weapons inspectors looked increas- ingly unlikely.

My final political meeting was to be with Naji Sabri al-Hadithi, the Western-educated Foreign Minister with a doctorate in English literature. Having previously headed up the Iraqi press office in London he was another Anglophile. During the Gulf War he was the Deputy Minister of Information and had kept his links with the ministry and the Iraqi press. It was probably through this connection that he had become a close friend of Saddam's younger son and heir apparent, Qusay.

Apart from our delegation I had also taken Caroline Horley to the meeting with me. Caroline is a BBC Middle East correspondent whom I had got to know well during the Bethlehem siege. She had very much wanted to meet with Naji Sabri, but the security people in the Ministry immediately recognised her and would not allow her into the meeting. The same happened with David Chancellor, the photographer who was travelling with us. As the meeting began, I asked why David and Caroline were not in the meeting. After asking again half an hour later, they were eventually allowed in.

This meeting proved to be more technical than the previous political meetings. There was precise talk of the nature of the weapons inspection. A long list was presented with names and information about the 257 proposed inspectors, along with some concern that they had not already arrived. Iraq had promised to fully cooperate with the inspection team, but they would not comply with further demands. It was at this point that we got onto the subject of terrorism and the "War on Terror."

Sabri stated emphatically that it was Iraq that started the war against terror, as for many years they had been the victims of Islamic terrorism, from both Whabbia and Shia groups. He stated that they knew how to deal with terrorists – they killed them. Fair enough, I thought, "That is certainly true." Iraq has killed thousands of terrorists. He continued to speak about the surrounding countries and how little some of them had done to overcome terrorism, before coming on to the subject of Iran.

The following day Naji Sabri was making a much-publicised visit to Iran, but despite this he continued to talk of the evil and dangerous nature of the Iranian regime. At some point he obviously realised that he had said too much, and asked us not to repeat what he had said. I had a private meeting with him once the delegation had left and again he stressed how this point must not be mentioned before he travelled to Tehran. After leaving the meeting I had three further calls from the ministry reiterating how important it was that his remarks were not repeated until he returned from Iran.

It was not the formal meetings, however, that I will remember from this visit. It was the quiet words that people began to say to me that were so poignant. Those who spoke were the military, diplomats and academics, people much respected in the higher echelons of Iraqi society. Their message this week was consistent.

The people of Iraq had suffered enough of the tyranny which had got them into this terrible state. They had been faithful servants but it had got them nowhere. They no longer wanted to be the enemy of the world.

As I sat one lunchtime in a military officers club, senior people spoke of how they were fed up with sanctions being used as an excuse for all of Iraq's problems and of how a few had in fact become very rich under the sanctions regime. People were sick of the lies and the terror that they all lived under. They spoke openly of the biological and chemical weapons programmes and of how it would be almost impossible for the weapons inspectors to find them.

They were all petrified of further war and yet their

assessment was that the only solution was for Saddam to go. They knew that this would not be possible without outside military intervention. This had been the constant theme of the week: "We need change and we need it quick."

As one who has dedicated his life to reconciliation and the attempt to bring peace and help overcome the suffering of the Iraqi people, I acutely felt the sense of failure. Over many months we had tried so hard and nothing had changed. The suffering had continued and the poverty had increased.

The infant mortality rate was now the highest in the world. The wards of the Al Mansour and Saddam Children's hospitals were still full of children dying of the most terrible malignancies. They still did not have proper pain control and despite the establishment of the bone marrow transplantation unit we knew that it would be an uphill struggle until the radiotherapy machines were repaired.

Back home the church was calling for further diplomacy. The world was crying out, "Stop the war" and here in Baghdad people were desperate for change. Desperate for change – but not for war. Late into the night that week, the two former army chaplains, Georges and I would talk about how this change might take place. We tried to think laterally about how war could be avoided while meeting the desires for change.

There were no easy answers. At times I wished that I was able to make statements from the safety of ignorance, which would now never be possible. Where was God in all of this and how does one discern his will in such great ethical complexities?

Chapter 8

Discerning What is Right in the Iraqi Crisis

As I sit and write in the safety of Clare College, Cambridge, all around is the talk of war or opposition to war. The church has not been silent in this issue but has spoken vigorously in defence of the people of Iraq. Theologians are debating whether war on Iraq falls into the criteria of a "just war." Most of the talk in favour of military action is about the threat of Iraq to the West.

This point is of particular concern to me because there is very little evidence that Iraq is a threat to the West. Iraq is a threat but primarily to its own people. They are the ones who have suffered so gravely and who continue to suffer. It is true that Iraq also poses a threat to Israel. As we saw in the last Gulf War, they were able to fire missiles indiscriminately into civilian Tel Aviv. Thankfully this was only with conventional warheads, but it is only one step further to use dirty weapons.

It is often said that you should never go to war unless it is worse not to go to war. What is defined as "worse" is very difficult. While the people of Iraq are desperate for change and an end to their suffering, none of them want war.

However hard I have tried, I can not come up with any methodology for changing the plight of the Iraqi people while its present leadership remains. However, this in itself does not justify war. There are major ethical dilemmas involved in one nation imposing regime change on another.

While I do not believe that the "just war" theory covers every eventuality, it must be taken seriously as an ethical starting point. The "just war" theory is an ancient Christian formula with its origins in the work of Thomas Aquinas and Augustine. It has many similarities to the Jewish formula for "just war" constituted by Maimonedes in the 13th century.

The theory has two main parts to it: *jus ad bellum* (the justice of going to war) and *jus in bello* (justice in wartime). In essence these theories look at when it can ever be right to go to war and how this should take place.

There are various versions of the "just war" theory but they tend to have six main points for *jus ad bellum*, and two for *jus in bellum*. A final part of this theory is *jus post bellum*, justice after war. This also needs to be achieved if there is to be any chance of war being seen as just and right morally.

The "Just War" Theory

Jus ad bellum

1. **Just cause**: The only reason for war is to prevent aggression or unjustified attack, or else to correct grave injustice.

2. **Competent authority**: Any force is only morally acceptable when it takes place with governmental authority, but in modern-day warfare only the support of the United Nations is seen as acceptable governmental authority.

3. **Limited objectives**: The goals of war must always be limited; therefore seeking to correct injustices cannot be without boundaries. It is imperative that the damage committed by war should be in proportion to the evil that the war is seeking to address.

4. **Right intention**: A war can only be judged to be just if it seeks to restore a just peace without ulterior motives.

5. **Last resort**: War should only be entered into after all means of diplomacy, negotiations or sanctions have been exhausted.

6. **Reasonable chance of success**: For a war to be seen as moral, it must always have a significant chance of reaching its end objective.

Jus in bello

1. **Proportionality**: The level of force used should be proportionate, in that it must be the minimum required to achieve the limited objectives of the war.

2. **Discrimination**: All effort should be made to avoid civilian casualties, with the main target of aggression being the military and perpetrators of the evil that is being fought.

Jus ad bellum (the justice of going to war)

Like all religious and philosophical theories with ancient routes, ascertaining the precise situations that constitute *just cause* is not an easy process. There must be intensive debate discussing the morality of any war but the situation of Iraq is particularly complex. There are a myriad of questions that need to be asked, not least whether it is possible to justify war on the grounds of the threat of a regime against its own people.

As I have already said, most of the present debate has to do with Iraq's threat to the world due to its supplies of weapons of mass destruction. The threat of Iraq to the world is minimal. Despite my clear objection to the whole sanctions regime, one cannot deny that Iraq is far less a threat to the world today than it was in 1990.

Nevertheless, while its ability to deliver biological or chemical weapons has been greatly reduced, there is significant information to show that Iraq continues to hold significant stocks of biological and chemical weapons. Over the past few months I have received countless reports of those involved in moving such toxic materials, often with catastrophic results. Some have died, and others have been left seriously incapacitated – including young officers cut down in their prime.

This is the other side to Iraq, that the people of Iraq have lived with for decades. These stories have only begun to be told to me within Iraq after many visits. The "just cause," if there is one, is not the threat of Iraq to the world but the threat of Iraq to its own people.

Since its inception, the United Nations has held a unique position in international law. What the UN says and decides is international law. It therefore has a key role to play in justifying *competent authority* in war. If the UN itself does not give its backing to particular military action it is difficult to justify the competent authority requirement.

However, there is increasing concern about the role of the UN in the international community, particularly where issues of the Middle East are concerned. The Islamic world has increasingly voted *en bloc*, bringing into question the methodology and ethics of some of the UN's decisions and even Security Council resolutions. Therefore the UN is not the only means by which the conditions of competent authority can be justified. A coalition of respected governments including the US and UK could easily argue that they with their limited allies do provide right authority.

When one comes to look at the issue of **limited objectives** there are further ambiguities in the Iraq situation. In the last Gulf War the objective was clear: the removal of Iraq from Kuwait. In the present conflict, however, there are two different messages being given out. One is the removal of weapons of mass destruction, and the other is the removal of the regime of Saddam Hussein. These are clearly two very different things, with very different methodologies required to bring about the end result.

If the grounds for war are simply the removal of weapons of mass destruction, we are onto complicated ethical grounds. Though we know with total certainty that Iraq does possess chemical and biological weapons, the risk of these weapons to the rest of the world is limited. Those at risk are primarily the people of Iraq and secondly the state of Israel. There is intelligence that Iraq had plans to use such weapons against Israel, which were thwarted because of the high probability that they would be shot down over other Arab nations before reaching their target. Iraq also was constrained by the fear that reprisals could involve non-conventional weapons.

With the increasing Islamisization of the conflict by Saddam Hussein there is also the risk that such weapons could fall into the hands of militant Islamic groups. As these groups engage in a major struggle against the West, they may have greater ability to use dirty weapons than Iraq. It must be reiterated, however, that the words of Tariq Aziz to me on 18 September 2001 are on the whole true. Iraq is not a terrorist nation but a revolutionary nation. The evil committed is in the name of the state and controlled by the state, and is not carried out at the hands of renegade vigilantes. As Naji Sabri stated to me in our last meeting, "Iraq has a way of dealing with terrorists, we kill them."

There is now an increasing belief in the international community that the real intention of the US and UK is actually regime change. It can be argued that regime change is the only way of guaranteeing that weapons of mass destruction are not produced again at a later date. Despite the issue of such weapons, the British Prime Minister Tony Blair has increasingly spoken of his concern for the Iraqi people. At Question Time in the House of Commons on 12 February 2003, he stated that the people of Iraq had suffered enough after twelve years of sanctions and that their suffering could not be allowed to continue indefinitely. This brings us to the issue of *right intention*. If a war is to be considered just, the intention must be to bring to an end a gross injustice without ulterior motives. The question of oil is one that people often have doubts about. Would we go to war with Iraq if it were not sitting on a significant percentage of the world's oil reserves? The likelihood, post-9/11, is yes. Afghanistan was not sitting on any great natural resources yet it was attacked because of its role in harbouring those involved in perpetrating terror.

There are also those who feel that the actions of George W. Bush are connected to the unfinished business of his father George Bush. Yet this issue itself may just be the result of a bizarre, but not unique, quirk of history. There are further ethical issues, including the length of time that the crisis with Iraq has been allowed to run on before a solution was found, causing such a severe humanitarian crisis. It could be argued that if this crisis had been dealt with earlier, we might not be in such a serious position as we are in today.

The reality is that the Gulf War in 1990–91 was not a "defining moment in history" as George Bush Sr said, but

9/11 was. The world is a very different place and the position of the US in the international community has grown even greater. Those attacks were seen not as just hitting three targets but the very heart of Western democracy and power.

"The War on Terrorism," though systemic, is being fought as a territorial war. This has major problems as well. It may result in the US failing to deal with the real "Axis of Evil" as they attempt to cleanse the world of rogue states. They could well miss the real target existing in the midst of their friends and allies. If the intention is to be right, and for war against Iraq to be seen as just, it must have to do with the liberation of the people of Iraq from tyranny, not just with the protection of the Western world.

The issue of the *last resort* has to be linked with right intention. If the intention is indeed to liberate the people of Iraq from such tyranny, then every other method has been tried and failed. Negotiations, sanctions and political pressure have failed to bring about a positive change in the nature of the regime.

It could be argued that the mechanisms that the West has used to contain and control Saddam Hussein since the last Gulf War have added considerably to the suffering of Iraq. If anything, they have increased the negative influence that the regime has had over its people. The sanctions system has meant that rations must be delivered in a well-organised, controlled way, which has given the Iraqi government an additional means of monitoring the whereabouts of its entire people. Those who do not turn up to purchase their rations are at risk of losing them permanently. Sanctions have unintentionally provided Saddam Hussein with an intelligence base in every corner shop.

If, however, the intention in this conflict is simply to do with weapons of mass destruction, then the issue of last resort is considerably different. In this scenario the recommendations of weapons inspectors must be paramount in any final decision to go to war.

There is no doubt that the combined US and British forces would have a very ***reasonable chance of success***, that is, if the intention is regime change. This does not mean that it is going to be easy to find Saddam Hussein, however. With seventy palaces, all of which prepare his evening meal every day, tracking him down will be like looking for a needle in a haystack, and there are of course hundreds of thousands of other places where he may stay.

The capture of Saddam at an early stage in any conflict is not however the determining factor in changing the regime. It is quite possible for there to be change prior to dealing with Saddam Hussein. The real question, however, is "At what price?" This leads us onto the issue of *jus in bellow* (justice in war).

Jus in bellow (*justice in war*)

War is always terrible. There is never such thing as a clean war, and all war is dirty, very dirty. Yet the just war theory does include ethical guide lines on the nature of war.

The degree of force used must be ***proportional*** to the end they are seeking to realize. Indiscriminate war is never justified. The level of force used must always be the minimum required to bring about the limited objectives of the war. That is why weapons which have an indiscriminate negative effect on future generations should always be avoided. The extreme case is in this genre is obviously nuclear weapons.

It could also be argued that the use of missiles covered in depleted uranium is ethically unacceptable. Their indiscriminate use in the last Gulf War has had a devastating effect, not just on those who were victims of attacks but also on

future generations. The high incidence of childhood malignancies and the increased levels of congenital deformities
bear witness to the use of ethically unacceptable weapons.
It has been argued that such pathology may also be the
result of the "toxic soup" released when bases containing
chemical and biological weapons were attacked. This simply
means that these weapons are also ethically unacceptable.

The second point of *jus in bellow* links in with the first.
Military action must not just show proportionality but it
must be **discriminate**. Where possible, attacks should only
target the political leadership and the military. The mass
bombing of World War II in cities such as Dresden was
totally contrary to the concept of *jus in bellow*, as is the
bombing of civilian infrastructure such as hospitals, schools
and places of worship.

Of course, this can be a difficult issue as evil regimes
may abuse civilian infrastructure or use civilians as human
shields at key military targets. This is precisely what happened in the last Gulf War, when Saddam Hussein placed his
"guests" in places of strategic significance such as dams,
military installations and satellite communication centres.
It has even been suggested that the terrible bombing of the
Amiria air raid shelter took place because on the roof was a
multiplicity of satellite communication equipment.

Whatever precautions are taken in war, there are always
casualties and it is never clean.

Jus post bellum (*justice after war*)

The final component of the just war theory deals with what
comes after war: ***jus post bellum***. The final outcome of
war needs to always to be the restoration of a lasting peace
and the establishment of a democratic rule. This needs to
happen within the cultural context of the defeated nation
and should not be about the establishment of a long-term

military rule which becomes an occupying force. In the case of Iraq, the restoration of the nation will necessitate a huge amount of inward investment and aid, in order to try and restore it merely to its pre-1991 position.

It must be appreciated that removing one dictatorial leader does not mean that there will not be others waiting to take his place. There is also a very real risk that following the overthrow of a dictatorial regime, those who have been oppressed may fight back with equal violence. This scenario occurred in the Balkans and other areas that experienced freedom for the first time in many years following the fall of communism.

The oppression of the Shia majority at the hands of a Sunni minority is of particular concern in Iraq. For years they have been oppressed at the hands of Saddam, and seen many of their leaders tortured or assassinated. Many have simply disappeared, as in the case of many of the Ayatollah Al Seder's family.

There are real fears of a backlash against the Christian minority, who may be regarded as having sided with Saddam Hussein, or as being part of the West, which in turn may be seen either as liberator or occupier. There is also a very real danger of further reprisals against Christians living in the Islamic world. Already there has been an increase in attacks against Christians since the "War on Terror" began.

Despite assurances from the West that this present war is not against Islam, most are not convinced. Almost all the countries and groups that are being targeted are Islamic and we are facing an increasing crisis between Islam and Christianity. This crisis, if not addressed, could result in the demise of the Church in much of the Islamic world.

It is imperative for the sake of the suffering Church that these Christians are given all the support that they need. But if we are to help secure their future long term, we need to encourage a new kind of dialogue which is not led by the Western inter-faith gurus of our age. It needs to be contextualised in the regions of conflict, and particularly in the Islamic world. Any dialogue must be based on truth which when combined with forgiveness can lead to reconciliation. The support of the Western Church is needed to enable and help facilitate such a process.

As we have seen, the theory of "just war" is complex and is not an accurate science. The situation of Iraq presents us with many ethical dilemmas, which every Christian needs to grapple with. We will all have different views, ideas and beliefs but I hope that this little book will help people to understand the complexities of this terrible crisis, not least by gaining some insight to the people on the ground in Iraq.

These are people like you and me, both Christians and Muslims. They are all victims, have all suffered and are all only one act away from execution. That applies not just to the people on the street but the people at the top, the Dr Umeed Mubarak and Jabbers of Iraq, who are part of the regime but also decent people who desperately care about the future of their citizens and nation.

Spiritual Reflections

The words of Psalm 137 have rung through my head continually as I have written these words.

> *"By the rivers of Babylon we sat down and there we wept*
> *when we remembered Zion . . .*
> *How can we sing the LORD's song in an alien [strange]*
> *land?"*   (RSV)

The people of Iraq once had their Zion, a life free of tyranny, starvation and suffering. Today there are fewer and fewer people who even remember those different days and yet they still struggle to sing the Lord's song.

I will never forget the night that I presented the Cross of Nails to the Evangelical Church of Baghdad. Every seat in the large church was filled. These people also suffered, but they were singing the Lord's song like I have never heard it sung before. The words of *"peace for the people of the Lord"* were followed by *"no eye has seen no ear has heard the wonder of our mighty God"* sung in Arabic. The faces of the people of God radiated his love. Many had tears in their eyes as they sang to the one who was their faithful friend in every trouble.

This experience has been repeated for me in countless places of worship in Iraq. Whether they be Chaldean, Syrian Orthodox or Evangelical, the people are still able to praise God. This is not to say that they do not fear or that they are exempt from the suffering of the nation. They have been able to fix their eyes on a spiritual future in another place, where one day they will be free from the sufferings of earthly life. As in the Negro spiritual songs of the past, they look forward to life on another shore.

The issues of theodicy are always real in such a crisis. Why does a God of love allow such evil? These were not the questions of Iraq's Christians; they know that their God is with them and loves them. What they have lost is not trust in God but in humanity. How can the human race fall to such a level to allow a whole nation to suffer so greatly?

Among the devastation of Iraq, time and time again one comes face to face with the image of God. The beauty of Ahmed and Immanuel, even in their disfigured bodies showing the love of Jesus. The poor family preparing a beautiful meal when they have almost nothing. The presence of hundreds in a damaged church without a minister, coming not to attend a service but simply to meet their Creator.

Then there was the most terrible and awful image of the woman holding her child blasted against the wall of the bombed air raid shelter. That image is the nearest thing I have ever seen to a soul, for it says that even though war may destroy the body you cannot destroy the soul.

I do not forget the Ayatollah Al Seder, for in him I also see God. He is a man not broken by the pressure, the one man who despite the huge political pressure on him will just speak of God and not enter in the myriad of words of the regime. Then there is the countless number of tiny emaci-ated children, dying in pain with their crying parents beside them. They also show the image of God because they are so close to being reunited with him.

Iraq is a nation I have grown to love, a people full of promise in a land of despair. It is a people of love in a nation of fear. Iraq is by tradition the setting of the Garden of Eden. It is a land full of promise, with water, sun, the world's greatest supply of dates and huge oil reserves, yet it can no longer feed its children. It is a nation whose people are attacked from within and from outside. It is a nation so hidden and so oppressed that when we talk of it we only think of war and terror, of an evil dictator and of political battles.

Night after night I have tried to think of how we can really help the people of Iraq. How we can find solutions to pending disaster and avoid further war and destruction? This morning as I wrote, I had a call from a Buddhist monk. He was on his way to Baghdad to be a human shield, as he also did in the last Gulf War. This time he has a letter in his pocket pleading with Saddam Hussein to leave the country for the sake of his people and nation. If only Saddam would do so ... but I do not believe he does really care for his people and nation. He loves only power and domination, a domination that will leave terrible scars on the land for many years to come.

Yet as I think of the Iraq I know, I realise that I also have been part of a people who have abused this once-great nation. The ancient land of Babylon, once the symbol of the oppressor of other nations, has become oppressed itself. My mind is taken back to the summer of 1999 when we presented the religious leaders of Iraq with the Coventry Cross of Nails. The plaque simply read *"To the people of Iraq. Father, forgive."*

It continues to be my prayer that our Father will forgive and have mercy on the people of Iraq. I have not presented answers but simply introduced you to a story of a journey to Baghdad and to the people good and bad. I have attempted to bring Iraq alive so that when you see those pictures on our television screen you too can say, "I have been there, I know those people, I pray for them and I also love them."

What is certain is that the people of faith in Iraq will not stop hoping, for their trust is in the Lord their Creator. As I walked through the moonlit streets of Baghdad one night with a Christian Iraqi friend, I asked him how he and his community kept going in the midst of such difficulties. He replied that it is by God's grace. He continued to answer by quoting from the final chapter of the book of Habakkuk:

> *"Though the fig tree does not bud*
>   *and there are no grapes on the vines,*
> *though the olive crop fails*
>   *and the fields produce no food,*
> *though there are no sheep in the pen*
>   *and no cattle in the stalls,*
> *yet I will rejoice in the* LORD,
>   *I will be joyful in God my Saviour."*

(Habakkuk 3:17–18)

As we walked back toward the Al Rasheed Hotel, I could see the tips of the swords of Saddam's victory parade, made from the shot-down Iranian planes. Towering over the skyline in the beauty of the moonlight, here good and evil met each other. I did not know what the future held for these people that I had grown to love so much. I knew that I would not be returning to the same Iraq. *I simply hoped that a horrible end might be better than unending horror*.

Nobody but God knows the future of Iraq. My prayer is that all people of faith may contribute to the rebuilding of that once great nation, that the Lord's song will be sung again in that strange land, and that peace will return.

If you have enjoyed this book and would like to help us to send a copy of it and many other titles to needy pastors in the **Third World**, please write for further information or send your gift to:

Sovereign World Trust
PO Box 777, Tonbridge
Kent TN11 0ZS
United Kingdom

or to the **'Sovereign World'** distributor in your country.

Visit our website at **www.sovereign-world.org**
for a full range of Sovereign World books.